Cambridge Elements

Elements in Eighteenth-Century Connections
edited by
Eve Tavor Bannet
University of Oklahoma
Markman Ellis
Queen Mary University of London

THE EPISTEMOLOGIES OF PROGRESS

Richard Adelman
University of Sussex

Shaftesbury Road, Cambridge CB2 8EA, United Kingdom

One Liberty Plaza, 20th Floor, New York, NY 10006, USA

477 Williamstown Road, Port Melbourne, VIC 3207, Australia

314–321, 3rd Floor, Plot 3, Splendor Forum, Jasola District Centre, New Delhi – 110025, India

103 Penang Road, #05–06/07, Visioncrest Commercial, Singapore 238467

Cambridge University Press is part of Cambridge University Press & Assessment, a department of the University of Cambridge.

We share the University's mission to contribute to society through the pursuit of education, learning and research at the highest international levels of excellence.

www.cambridge.org
Information on this title: www.cambridge.org/9781009614207
DOI: 10.1017/9781009614191

© Richard Adelman 2025

This publication is in copyright. Subject to statutory exception and to the provisions of relevant collective licensing agreements, no reproduction of any part may take place without the written permission of Cambridge University Press & Assessment.

When citing this work, please include a reference to the DOI 10.1017/9781009614191

First published 2025

A catalogue record for this publication is available from the British Library

ISBN 978-1-009-61420-7 Hardback
ISBN 978-1-009-61418-4 Paperback
ISSN 2632-5578 (online)
ISSN 2632-556X (print)

Cambridge University Press & Assessment has no responsibility for the persistence or accuracy of URLs for external or third-party internet websites referred to in this publication and does not guarantee that any content on such websites is, or will remain, accurate or appropriate.

For EU product safety concerns, contact us at Calle de José Abascal, 56, 1°, 28003 Madrid, Spain, or email eugpsr@cambridge.org

The Epistemologies of Progress

Elements in Eighteenth-Century Connections

DOI: 10.1017/9781009614191
First published online: May 2025

Richard Adelman
University of Sussex
Author for correspondence: Richard Adelman, r.adelman@sussex.ac.uk

Abstract: *The Epistemologies of Progress* brings together two recent critical trends to offer a new understanding of Scottish-Enlightenment narratives of progress. The first trend is the new consideration of the ambiguities inherent in eighteenth-century thought on this subject. The second is the fast-growing body of scholarship identifying the surprising role of scepticism in Enlightenment philosophy across Europe. The author's analysis demonstrates that stadial history is best understood through the terms of contemporary scepticism, and that doing so allows for the identification of structural reasons why such thought has been characterized by its ambiguities. Seen in this light, contemporary accounts of progress form a spectrum of epistemological rigour. At one end of this spectrum all knowledge is self-reflexively recognized to be analogy, surmise, 'speculation', and 'conjecture', untethered from lay-conceptions facticity. At the other end stand quotidian political claims, but made alongside reference to the sceptical conception of knowledge and argumentation.

Keywords: scepticism, progress, Scottish enlightenment, epistemology, Ossian

© Richard Adelman 2025

ISBNs: 9781009614207 (HB), 9781009614184 (PB), 9781009614191 (OC)
ISSNs: 2632-5578 (online), 2632-556X (print)

Contents

Introduction   1

1 James Dunbar and the 'Instinctive Propensities'
   of Lay Knowledge   11

2 John Millar and the Certainties of Colonialism   23

3 Ossian and the Biases of Commercial Modernity   38

   Conclusion   54

   Bibliography   60

Introduction

The key thinkers of the Scottish Enlightenment have long been recognized as not entirely sanguine on the question of social progress. Observations across the canon of contemporary moral philosophy, including stadial history and political economy, on the potential for moral degradation generated by commercial society, are the obvious basis for this position. Critical attention to the apparent downsides of so-called social evolution in such thought seems to have increased in recent years, however. David Spadafora, in his seminal 1990 *The Idea of Progress in Eighteenth-Century Britain*, which refocused scholarly attention from contemporary French to British theorists of social progress, took up what was then a broadly shared stance on these issues. Noting the evidence that the 'Scottish *literati* of the eighteenth century' followed Jean-Jacques Rousseau and 'did not really believe in progress', Spadafora tidies away these issues to conclude that 'on the whole the Scots *did* consider the pattern of development that they discerned in history to be broadly progressive', and that it is both 'necessary' and 'historically correct' to emphasize this progressive aspect to their thought.[1] John Regan, by contrast, considering similar texts and issues in 2014, summarizes the whole terrain of later eighteenth-century thought concerning progress through what he sees as its consistent ambiguities. The 'nuances of stadialism', for Regan, are engendered by the 'defining ambiguity in stadial history', the 'tension between an inherent progressiveness and deterioration in human development'.[2] No doubt this shift, which is evidenced across recent criticism,[3] stems in part from the political climate in which this work has been composed. As Jordana Rosenberg and Chi-ming Yang put it, also in 2014,

> [i]n our contemporary moment, the redoubled attacks on the poor and working classes, and the intensification of state violence that has been waged under the cover of claims to restore economic 'stability' since the punctual crisis of 2008, call out for a sustained inquiry into the historical dimensions of capitalist production – with its attendant crises and violent consolidations

---

[1] Spadafora, *The Idea of Progress*, p. 254, n. 2.
[2] Regan, 'Ambiguous Progress and Its Poetic Correlatives', 615–34 (621 & 622). My argument in this study is in part complementary to Regan's. Regan recovers, through analysis of Thomas Percy's *Reliques of Ancient English Poetry* (1767), how mid-century literary editing, like contemporary history, was 'alive to the significance of writing as an index to human progress' (p. 615). My analysis of James Macpherson and Hugh Blair also tends in the same direction, but focuses on reconstructing the sceptical epistemology such critical and historical tasks involve.
[3] Cf. Palmeri, *State of Nature*, Perelman, *The Invention of Capitalism*, Sebastiani, *The Scottish Enlightenment*, and Wengrow & Graeber, *The Dawn of Everything*, the last of which counters the simplistic readings of stadial history from the eighteenth century to the present with the non-linear and not-simply progressive account of human social difference that has emerged from the last few decades' archaeology and anthropology.

of power and resources – as well as the mediations of these phenomena in aesthetic form.[4]

While Rosenberg and Yang are referring to recent criticism of eighteenth-century 'dispossession', their summary applies just as neatly to accounts of the ideologies of progress that entwine with, or sometimes underpin, such representations. 'Improvement', of course, was the watchword of eighteenth-century enclosure.

Occurring at the same time as this shift towards reconsidering the apparent pitfalls of social progress, a distinct but related branch of scholarship has begun the task of re-evaluating the substructural epistemologies of Enlightenment thought across Europe. Outside of this new branch of scholarship, Enlightenment philosophers are most often considered confident empiricists who develop 'scientific' methodologies to grasp the fundamental nature of individual and social life. Clifford Siskin, for example, in his book *System: The Shaping of Modern Knowledge* (2016), argues that 'system' itself, and 'scalable' systematic thinking, are the primary 'technologies' of Enlightenment thought, the ones that enable it to 'shape knowledge' into a useful form, to give philosophers the 'confidence that the world could be known', and to generate a 'science' of man.[5] This position is representative of a school of criticism that finds in Enlightenment philosophy an epoch-making, proto-modern set of practices and of political positions, with socio-economic progress at their heart.[6] Working against these claims, however, recent inquiries into the status of philosophical scepticism in Enlightenment thought have challenged the extent to which this field anticipates 'scientific' developments, and the extent to which it exhibits a confident and coherent empiricism. Anton Matytsin's (2016) *The Specter of Skepticism in the Age of Enlightenment*, for example, demonstrates that thinkers of a variety of disciplinary and ideological affiliations, across France, Switzerland, the Dutch Republic, and Prussia, accommodated and incorporated sceptical claims in their writing. In Matytsin's account, the sceptical deconstruction of quotidian models of knowledge – that processes of causation are inaccessible to the human mind, and that the human senses do not provide verifiable knowledge of the world – was effectively considered unanswerable, across European thought, by the mid eighteenth century. John Christian Laursen and Gianni Paganini's collection *Skepticism and Political Thought in the Seventeenth and Eighteenth Centuries* (2015) similarly identifies the extensive level of engagement with sceptical philosophy across two

---

[4] Rosenberg & Yang, 'The Dispossessed Eighteenth Century', 137–52 (137).
[5] Siskin, *System*, pp. 2 & 41.
[6] See, for instance, Schliesser, *Adam Smith* and Schabas & Wennerlind, *A Philosopher's Economist*.

centuries of highly varied European political thought, from François de La Mothe Le Vayer, the tutor to Louis XVI, to Carl Friedrich Stäudlin, the post-Kantian moral philosopher.[7]

The present study aims to connect, combine and further the insights of these two waves in recent scholarship – renewed critical attention to the ambivalences at the heart of eighteenth-century conceptions of progress, and isolations of the scepticism at play in Enlightenment thought. By doing so, the analysis that follows reveals that the negative consequences attendant on commercial progress stated by Scottish writers are in fact just a set of secondary manifestations of a more fundamental ambivalence concerning the very nature of human social enquiry. This is because contemporary sociopolitical claims are constructed through genres of knowledge dictated by the period's underlying scepticism. Such claims thus include, as part and parcel of their expression and existence, the idea that they stand at a considerable remove from certainty, or from evidence-based factuality. The ambivalence they express is not just political or personal, but epistemological and structural, in other words. Further, the contemporary modes of knowledge able to be applied to questions of progress should be understood, I contend, as positions on a spectrum, ranging from a high level of epistemological rigour and a pronounced self-reflexivity concerning the status of their claims, at one end, to a loose reference to the same model of knowledge combined with more quotidian political claims at the other. The materials considered here are chosen first, to illustrate how ambivalence concerning progress is thus part of the very fabric of eighteenth-century socio-philosophical and historical enquiry, a field which has stadial history at its heart; and second, to exemplify three different positions on the epistemological spectrum contemporary scepticism creates. The texts under consideration also come from the most significant moment of the Scottish *literati*'s collective inquiry into progress, the period between 1760 and the early 1780s. It is at the beginning of this period that the terms of the dominant version of stadial history are coined, by Adam Smith, in his *Lectures on Jurisprudence* (1762–3 and 1766). And it is also the last moment, and highpoint, of such epistemologically sophisticated, self-conscious inquiry, before the waning of the dominion of scepticism over European thought, which begins in the late 1770s, allows less cautious ideological positions on the question of progress to become dominant.[8]

---

[7] See also Matytsin & Burston (eds.), *The Skeptical Enlightenment*, and Griswold, 'Philosophy and Skepticism', pp. 147–78. My own work has also contributed to this field; cf. Adelman, *Doubtful Knowledge*.

[8] Michel Foucault identified this tectonic shift in the nature of knowledge in his 1966 *The Order of Things*, claiming that the first signs of this vast 'rupture' were visible in 1775 (p. 221). The recent identifications of the centrality of scepticism to Enlightenment thought have augmented our

The first section of this Element thus considers a representative, though little-discussed example of the full epistemological rigour concerning human social enquiry, James Dunbar's *Essays on the History of Mankind in Rude and Cultivated Ages* (1780). Dunbar's erudite and precise style, reminiscent of Adam Ferguson's prose, repeatedly recaps the contemporary sceptical model of knowledge so as to apply its procedures and insights to the issue of progress. His title's chosen terms, 'rude' and cultivated', indeed, are revealed in the course of his analysis as references to such epistemological precision. The second section of the Element turns to John Millar's *The Origin of the Distinction of Ranks* (1771), which also performs, in many respects, orthodox sceptical analysis. Millar's modifications to his text after its initial publication, however, evidence striking movement away from epistemological precision, towards something more akin to a political ideology of progress. These modifications also overtly ignore his contemporaries' analysis of modern European ideological bias, seemingly because the stance they promote stands uncomfortably close to that commonplace position. The final section of the Element turns to the critical writing, from the mid-1760s, by James Macpherson and Hugh Blair, concerning the reputed ancient Scottish bard Ossian. These texts are contemporary with Adam Smith's coinage of the dominant categories of contemporary stadial history, and indeed – like Dunbar's and Millar's analyses – also suggest their own versions of such stages. Ultimately however, they represent a third position on the contemporary spectrum of epistemological rigour, making extended reference to that model of knowledge, but repeatedly sidestepping the issues germane to historical evidence to which that model draws attention, so as to configure Ossian's poetry as a unique specimen in the otherwise vexed field of historical knowledge.

The present analysis thus refocuses attention from the question of whether individual philosophers are apologists for progress, to how contemporary parameters of knowledge informed, configured, and allowed for a distinct variety of handlings of the issue of social difference. Arranging these different treatments of the ideas of progress in order of their epistemological rigour, as opposed to their chronological order, allows the analysis that follows to trace most clearly how contemporary discourse deviates – either strategically or unconsciously – from a shared body of methodological tenets. For the epistemological subtleties found in Dunbar's analysis are in fact representative of the sceptical norms of the period's philosophy. The stakes in such analysis are clearly high. Joseph S. Lucas records, for instance, how texts by just a handful

---

understanding of the epistemological conditions before this 'rupture', but the shift towards a new, empirical 'episteme' Foucault identifies remains convincing.

of mid eighteenth-century Scots addressing the questions of social evolution 'wielded an enormous influence on late eighteenth-century thought', and became 'known to educated readers throughout the British Empire'.[9] Scottish-Enlightenment thought concerning social difference, in other words, came to hold a foundational position in the later ideologies of colonialism. Isolating the epistemological conditions informing eighteenth-century analysis of social difference thus serves to complicate and add significant nuance to the proto-racial and intercultural judgements at the heart of colonialism. Furthermore, approaching and arranging contemporary analyses in epistemological, rather than chronological, order also offers a new means of classifying and indeed understanding the different political positions that are available in this influential strand of mid to late eighteenth-century thought.

A clear example of the epistemological nuance of such claims (summarized from my own analysis of scepticism's role in contemporary political economy) is visible in Adam Smith's *Lectures on Jurisprudence*, in the earlier student report of his lectures, which hold the first record of Smith's account of both the terms of stadial history and 'the division of labour'. These two concepts both stand at the centre of contemporary Scottish philosophy's model of social progress based on economic stages. By the early nineteenth century, they also come to be closely interwoven with the logics of empire.[10] But Smith does not introduce either concept to his Glasgow students in such a way as to make it the key to social evolution. On the contrary, taking the division of labour first, Smith introduces this as the only heuristic category that can make the in-fact perplexing issue of global social difference make any sense. In an extended comparison between the 'way of life' of a 'savage' and that of an 'ordinary day-labourer in England or Holland', that is, Smith dwells at some length on the many reasons it is difficult to make a judgement on which mode of life might be seen as better.[11] Thus, Smith notes that 'every savage has the full enjoyment of the fruits of his own labours; there are there no landlords, no usurers, no tax gatherers';[12] but

---

[9] Lucas, 'The Course of Empire and the Long Road to Civilization', 166–90 (169).
[10] See, for example, Ricardo, *Principles*, 2 vols., I: 100, n. 1: 'In some countries of Europe, and many of Asia, as well as in the islands in the South Seas, the people are miserable, either from a vicious government or from habits of indolence, which make them prefer present ease and inactivity, though without security against want, to a moderate degree of exertion, with plenty of food and necessaries. By diminishing their population, no relief would be afforded, for productions would diminish in as great, or even in a greater, proportion. The remedy for the evils under which Poland and Ireland suffer, which are similar to those experienced in the South Seas, is to stimulate exertion, to create new wants, and to implant new tastes; for those countries must accumulate a much larger amount of capital, before the diminished rate of production will render the progress of capital necessarily less rapid than the progress of population.'
[11] Smith, 'Report of 1762-3', pp. 1–394 (p. 340).   [12] Ibid.

also that the 'indigence of a savage is far greater than that of the meanest citizen of any thing that deserves the name of a civilized nation'.[13] Moreover, for Smith, '[t]here is another consideration which increases the difficulty in accounting for' the difference between these modes of life.[14] This is the high proportion of civilized citizens who do not labour, but instead live off the labour of others. This situation is so marked, indeed, that Smith expresses it quite violently: 'The labour and time of the poor is in civilized countries sacrificed to the maintaining the rich in ease and luxury'.[15] (This claim also stands at the base of Smith's published remark, in the later *Wealth of Nations*, of 1776, that '[c]ivil government [...] is in reality instituted for the defence of the rich against the poor'.[16])

Thus, after a long section of this lecture detailing these complexities, and showing directly how they stand in the way of any explanation of the difference between the categories of 'savage' and 'civilized' – to such an extent indeed that these terms themselves are made to seem highly problematic – Smith reveals his solution: 'In what manner then shall we account for the great share [the day-labourer] and the lowest of the people have of the conveniencies [sic] of life. [sic] The division of labour amongst different hands can alone account for this.'[17] Note then, that Smith's phrase 'can alone account' renders the division of labour a necessary limitation of the factors of his discussion to allow explanation to proceed. (He goes on, after this quotation, to offer an account of specialization beginning with 'pin-making', like that found in the *Wealth of Nations*.) But yet what the division of labour 'accounts' for here is only 'the great share' that common people have in 'the conveniencies of life' in so-called civilized society. The many other qualities of life Smith's account brought to attention – such as the savage's 'full enjoyment of the fruits of his own labours', or the 'sacrifice' of the 'labour and time' of the poor within civilization – are thus left off-stage and unaccounted for. Social difference as it occurs across the eighteenth-century globe remains a perplexingly fraught subject, in other words, even if the issue of 'conveniencies' allows for a relatively neat and satisfying – but an avowedly limited – explanation.

Because this same issue plays out at length in Smith's mature rendering of these issues, both in the *Wealth of Nations* and in that text's 'Early Draft',[18] and because the self-consciously precise and limited nature of these claims is a frequent occurrence across contemporary socio-philosophical thought, it would be a mistake to consider Smith's remarks around the 'division of labour' here as a solid claim about social evolution, or about cultural superiority *tout*

---

[13] Ibid., p. 341.   [14] Ibid.   [15] Ibid., p. 340.   [16] Smith, *Wealth of Nations*, 2 Vols., II: 715.
[17] Smith, 'Report of 1762–3', p. 341.
[18] See Adelman, 'Doubtful Knowledge in the *Wealth of Nations*', *Doubtful Knowledge*.

court, let alone as a proto-racial claim regarding different peoples' capacities or tendencies. Even through the probable imprecision of student note-taking, indeed, Smith seems careful to introduce his four stages of human society ('1st, the Age of Hunters; 2dly, the Age of Shepherds; 3dly, the Age of Agriculture; and 4^{thly}, the Age of Commerce') as an imaginative supposition rather than certainty.[19] Furthermore, Smith's published writing, both before and after the *Lectures*, in complete accord with the climate of contemporary philosophy in both France and Scotland, evidences what I have described elsewhere as his co-creation of a distinct proto-psychology, and of a political ideology, that are both grounded in the terms of contemporary philosophical scepticism. A key feature of this ideology is distrust over the bias and hubris implicit in modern Europeans' judgements of different social modes. And because Smith and his contemporaries self-reflexively highlight their own participation in such bias, their sceptical mode of moral philosophy emphasizes what Laursen and Paganini term contemporary scepticism's 'suspended judgement' on such intercultural and political matters, and refuses to conduct inquiries into social difference with anything approaching certainty.[20]

The shared, proto-psychological model that gives rise to these political stances is one in which human knowledge is configured as a series of inevitably false surmises. They are 'false', because sceptical reasoning can pinpoint the consistent mismatch between our sense data and the material parameters of the real world. Smith, for example, illustrates this, in his posthumously published 'External Senses' essay, by reference to the gap between the sense data that tells the human mind that the earth is stationary and the philosophical reasoning which shows that the planet is actually 'in motion [...] with a rapidity that almost passes all human comprehension'.[21] Items of knowledge, likewise, are 'surmises', because they approximate, in significantly simplified terms, phenomena that the human mind cannot fully access. This predicament, moreover, applies even to quotidian, commonplace perceptions, and even to knowledge of the self, which is effectively projected, and 'feign[ed]' (to use David Hume's term), from patchy, always-incomplete, and always-limited, sense-data.[22] And it applies, in equally total terms, to historical reasoning, especially that

---

[19] Smith, 'Report of 1762–3', p. 14. On how Smith's stadial terms are imaginative supposition, see, for example, p. 14, where the notes have Smith introducing the scenario overtly as a hypothetical – 'If we should suppose 10 or 12 persons of different sexes settled in an uninhabited island ...' – and p. 22, where a doubled 'probably' in the student notes point towards careful hedging in Smith's delivery: 'The first origin of private property would probably be mens [sic] taking themselves to fixt [sic] habitations and living together in cities, which would probably be the case in every improved society.'

[20] Laursen and Paganini, 'Introduction' to *Skepticism and Political Thought in the Seventeenth and Eighteenth Centuries*, pp. 3–16 (3–4).

[21] Smith, 'Of the External Senses', pp. 135–70 (p. 137);   [22] Hume, *Treatise*, p. 209.

concerning pre-history. In the *Wealth of Nations*, for example, Smith reminds his reader that the whole of pre-classical history is lacking 'any distinct or circumstantial account', by naming the 'fall of the Greek republics and of the Persian empire' as 'the first great revolution in the affairs of mankind' for which we have such evidence.[23]

In terms of an individual's perception, what contemporary scepticism says about this seeming impasse is that it is also 'natural', and indeed inevitable (even for the sceptic him- or herself) to act as if this impasse didn't exist. So people consider their surmises and projections concerning the external world (and concerning the self) to be factually, physically true. And although the mind can sustain a mode of sceptical — technically correct — insight for short periods, natural human mental tendencies do not allow anyone to proceed in that manner for any length of time. Smith dramatizes this, self-reflexively and comically, in his 'Astronomy' essay, and also in his Glasgow lectures.[24] Other writing in this tradition — recent scholarship has identified the reigning sceptical epistemology as operating in shared terms across Europe, and especially in France — emphasizes the thirst for the feeling of certainty that all humans experience, even where real knowledge is an impossibility.[25] In terms of the wider project of human social knowledge, contemporary scepticism's chosen procedures are to deploy repeat caveats regarding the vexed status of its claims, and to make use of genres of knowledge that overtly advertise their artificially constructed nature. Together, these strategies make the total non-factuality of such thought as clear as possible to their readers. Rousseau, for instance, who Spadafora glosses as simply not believing in progress, actually introduces his

---

[23] Smith, *Wealth of Nations*, II: 702.

[24] See Adam Smith, 'The History of Astronomy', in *Essays on Philosophical Subjects*, ed. W. P. D. Wightman & J. C. Bryce (Oxford: Oxford University Press, 1978), pp. 33–105 (p. 105): 'And even we, while we have been endeavouring to represent all philosophical systems as mere inventions of the imagination, to connect together the otherwise disjointed and discordant phenomena of Nature, have insensibly been drawn in, to make use of language expressing the connecting principles of this one, as if they were the real chains which Nature makes use of to bind together her several operations.' Cf. Smith, 'Report of 1762–3', p. 352: 'Men always endeavour to persuade others to be of their opinion even when the matter is of no consequence to them. If one advances any thing concerning China or the *more distant moon* [emphasis original] which contradicts what you imagine to be true, you immediately try to persuade him to alter his opinion.'

[25] In Scotland, James Steuart offers one of countless examples of this, in his *Inquiry into the Principles of Political Oeconomy*, II, 441: 'I must observe, that all short sketches of this kind are intended only to satisfy a general curiosity which mankind has, to know a little of every thing. Although they may appear superficial and incorrect, to persons thoroughly instructed in those matters, they still are [*sic*] for our purpose; which is only to take them as something approaching nearer to truth than bare suppositions can do'. For the wider European context, see Matytsin, *The Specter of Skepticism*; for analysis of contemporary French scepticism, see Adelman, *Doubtful Knowledge*, Chapter 2.

Discours sur l'origine et les fondements de l'inégalité parmi les hommes (*Discourse on the origins and foundations of inequality among men*), of 1755, by clarifying the limited nature of such an enquiry into the unrecorded and therefore unknowable human past. He thus 'set[s] aside all facts', depicts his text as 'not' a 'pursuit of the truths of history', and instead classifies it as a series of 'conjectures'.[26] He also cautions his readers to 'not imagine' that he 'flatters' himself 'as having seen what' he 'believe[s] to be so difficult to see'.[27] When one understands statements such as these as representative of the contemporary philosophical method regarding human social enquiry in the face of seemingly unanswerable sceptical analysis, Spadafora's aside that Rousseau does not 'believe' in progress can be seen as a limited assessment of what is in fact a wider and more complex epistemological and political context. (Rousseau's reference to 'facts' is normally glossed, rather unsatisfactorily, as one to Biblical authority.[28])

Rousseau's term 'conjecture' is a key epistemological signpost, here. It stands behind the genre of analysis that comes to be called 'conjectural history', in the 1790s, but which is earlier termed 'natural history'. The most common way of reading conjectural history, in recent criticism, is as indistinguishable from evidence-based argumentation, and also as expressions of its author's 'beliefs'. Spadafora's comments on Rousseau are not unusual therefore. Summarizing a wider range of contemporary related ideas, for instance, Spadafora also has recourse to such authors' 'views' and 'belief':

> Varieties of pessimism undoubtedly constituted a more than negligible portion of the historical outlook of the eighteenth century. But their force was limited in important ways throughout the period. A number of primitivists, for instance, held their critical views of modern civilization in an uneasy tension with a belief in progress.[29]

Roxann Wheeler, in her full and erudite account of the diversity of eighteenth-century thought concerning race and 'complexion', makes use of similar formulations when it comes to the writings of natural history:

> Although most British natural historians subscribed to Christian beliefs, they propounded a secular rationale of differences among people in their writings. These natural differences, they believed, arose from geographic variation, climatic conditions, and a people's related cultural habits.[30]

The same gesture occurs here: 'In this model, human characteristics, they believed, were formed over time by external forces working on the

---

[26] Rousseau, *Inequality*, p. 78.   [27] Ibid., p. 68.
[28] See, for instance, Palmeri, *State of Nature*, pp. 4–5.
[29] Spadafora, *The Idea of Progress*, p. 16.   [30] Wheeler, *The Complexion of Race*, p. 22.

body.'[31] Wheeler thus considers contemporary stadial history – the supposition of the 'four stages' coined by Smith – to be 'undergird[ed]' by 'a belief in the progress and the perfectibility of society' and ultimately concludes that 'natural historians and proponents of the secular four-stages theory, shared the ethnocentric belief that England – and much of Europe – was the best place on earth'![32] Such comments run counter to the fraught picture of social difference we saw Smith emphasize. They also stand in stark contrast to the pervasive cultural relativism, and the awareness of the ideological biases of modern Europeans, visible in contemporary moral philosophy once one identifies its substructural scepticism.

Frank Palmeri's more recent, book-length treatment of the conjectural form offers a more careful and accurate understanding of its terms – again in accordance with the shifting critical emphasis towards the ambiguities at the heart of eighteenth-century discourses. Contextualizing conjectural history via its historical developments (since classical antiquity) and by its national variations (it is used differently across Europe, he claims), Palmeri recognizes that the genre's central verbal formulations convey neither certainty nor belief:

> The genre of conjectural history signals its distinctive temporality through the use of what could be called the 'conjectural necessary' form of the past. This form figures prominently in speculative assertions of what 'must have' occurred in the past, given the current state of our knowledge. Such formulations differ from the past perfect or the simple past, the statement of what 'had' happened before what happened. At first sight, the assertion that a certain development 'must have' taken place at a certain point may appear to be more definite than these other assertions of past occurrences. But the 'must have' harbors in its assertion of necessity a doubt of actuality. The past that is so predicated 'must have' happened because we do not know if it 'did' take place.[33]

Palmeri here makes a useful distinction between the emphatic certainty that appears to reign in conjectural history at first glance, and the significantly more nuanced and provisional position that is in fact engendered when one understands the form's intellectual procedures. Palmeri also approvingly quotes the figure who named the term, Dugald Stewart, for distancing the contents of such conjectural accounts from factuality: 'But whether the conjectured events actually occurred is not the question: "it is more important to ascertain the progress that is most simple than the progress that is most agreeable to fact; for paradoxical as the proposition may appear, it is certainly true, that the real progress is not always the most natural"'.[34] Stewart, I have argued, is summarizing conjectural history's mode of argumentation from

---

[31] Ibid. [32] Ibid., pp. 35 & 37. [33] Palmeri, *State of Nature*, p. 16. [34] Ibid., p. 7.

within the sceptical tradition, defending it against falsely empirical readings. The reigning sceptical epistemology now becoming visible in European Enlightenment thought therefore adds a further layer of epistemological and political contextualization to Palmeri's already thorough account. For what Palmeri terms conjectural history's 'doubt of actuality' is the ideal mode of inquiry for eighteenth-century sceptical moral philosophy, with its central dictum that human knowledge cannot escape its predicament of surmise, analogy, approximation, and simplification. The subtle, tentative suggestions of what 'must have' taken place, are thus doubly hedged as doubtful, but as perhaps-useful, when the form is used from within a work propounding sceptical principles, or indeed from within an intellectual culture, like that of the Scottish Enlightenment, proceeding in accordance with a largely shared model of sceptical analysis.

The present study therefore contends that this same set of intellectual coordinates informs – to varying degrees – contemporary stadial history and that mode's claims concerning progress. In what follows, I trace the intricate dynamics of three examples of Scottish stadial, conjectural history. While Macpherson and Blair's Ossian writings are not normally placed in this group, I demonstrate their epistemological and political consanguinity with it, not least because of the two figures' interest in using the evidence of Ossian's poetry to coin new stages through which human history might pass. At times, indeed, this socio-philosophical, conjectural endeavour can seem like the primary purpose of the Ossian publications. I contend throughout this analysis that it is contemporary scepticism that provides the key to understanding both the often careful and poised claims at issue in stadial history and also the digressions from such subtlety that this body of work also includes. In the texts considered here, indeed, the latter evidences knowledge of sceptical argumentative methodologies as much as the former.

1 James Dunbar and the 'Instinctive Propensities' of Lay Knowledge

James Dunbar has not been the subject of much critical attention, and might therefore seem quite peripheral to Scottish-Enlightenment thought. In fact however, Dunbar, who taught moral philosophy at King's College, Aberdeen between 1765 and 1794, engages at a high level of sophistication with many of the shared concerns of his more studied contemporaries. He makes extensive reference to the writings of Adam Ferguson and Adam Smith, for example, while also offering significant extensions to both these figures' ideas, in his 1780 *Essays on the History of Mankind in Rude and Cultivated Ages*. Paul

Wood has also recorded Dunbar's participation in the Aberdeen Philosophical Society that was active between 1758 and 1773, the highest proportion of the meetings of which, after criticism, considered epistemology and natural history. For Wood, Dunbar's *Essays* had their origin in these meetings and in their wide-ranging considerations of contemporary intellectual culture.[35]

The *Essays* introduce their reflections on the questions pertaining to social progress by drawing precise attention to the vexed nature of knowledge in the sphere of human history. This is a rhetorical strategy pioneered by Hume and also followed by Ferguson and by James Steuart. Dunbar thus first classifies his text as a self-consciously 'loose' series of 'essays', so as to evade the problems of 'systematic arrangement' and 'philosophic theory'.[36] These terms allude to the problem of the false allure of 'systems' of thought that contemporary scepticism describes: systems are the result of the human thirst for certainty, but in fact multiply simplistic principles and twist evidence in accordance with their necessarily limited 'hypothesis' or 'theory'. The self-consciously 'loose' essay form represents the solution to such problems followed in Scotland since Hume, because it renders knowledge momentary, variable, conditional, and overtly non-cumulative. (Wood notes that Hume's thought was a 'disproportionately large' focus of the Aberdeen Philosophical Society, and that the group's most famous member, Thomas Reid, ironically remarked to Hume that 'If you write no more in morals[,] politicks or metaphysicks, I am affraid [*sic*] we shall be at a loss for Subjects'.[37]) With this model of the potential pitfalls of human knowledge sketched, Dunbar can apply it to the issues of human social history. It is thus, for Dunbar, a great 'pity' that the 'transactions' of 'primeval' life are 'consigned to eternal oblivion', as such knowledge, if it were possible, 'would reflect a light upon moral and political science' (*Essays*, p. 1). The purpose of highlighting this impasse is to explain the necessity of the conjectural mode: 'Consistently, however, with present appearances, and with the memorials of antiquity, the following changes, it is pretended, may have arisen successively to the species' (*Essays*, p. 2). Dunbar's text, in other words, is framed here as a natural history, as a series of conjectures, of what 'may have arisen' in the distant human past, in full acknowledgement of the vast chasm between that task and either evidence or certainty, and in full acknowledgement of the tendencies of the human intellect towards falsely totalizing 'theory'. The term 'pretend' here, we might note, invokes, even in its eighteenth-century uses, what the *OED* terms 'make-believe', 'simulation', and

---

[35] Wood, 'Aberdeen Philosophical Society'.
[36] Dunbar, *Essays on the History of Mankind in Rude and Cultivated Ages*, p. i (hereafter cited parenthetically as *Essays*).
[37] Wood, 'Aberdeen Philosophical Society'.

'feign[ing]'. Three of Samuel Johnson's four definitions of the term in 1773, for example, connote falsity.

Still at this stage of framing the intellectual exercise of the *Essays*, Dunbar therefore posits – against Smith's earlier categories of subsistence, and as his provisional, suppositional claim – three stages of social history in which the human figure 'may be contemplated': first, 'in a separate and individual state, before the date of language' (*Essays*, p. 2); second, 'a proficient in language, and a member of that artless community which consists with equality, with freedom, and independence' (*Essays*, p. 2); and third, 'under the protection and discipline of civil government' (*Essays*, p. 3). But even more directly than his earlier contemporaries, Dunbar is careful to stipulate that the 'order' of these imagined scenes is entirely heuristic rather than real: 'But it is the order of improvement merely, not the chronological order of the world, that belongs to this enquiry' (*Essays*, p. 3). This formulation, importantly, moves Dunbar's conjectures further away from the repeat implication made by Smith, by Rousseau and by others, in their handling of parallel materials, that the logic of human stages reveals a one-way dynamic in the history of humankind. While it is common, across the eighteenth century, as Spadafora notes, to stress the potential for degeneracy from a seeming high-point of 'civilized' development, Dunbar's gesture here of signalling the problematic simplicity of linear claims themselves extends the sceptical distrust of human knowledge-formations even further across the project of conjectural history. The writing of conjectural history itself is therefore acknowledged here as a process of speculative simplification and abstraction. Perhaps paradoxically to modern eyes, Dunbar is thus proceeding with this intellectual exercise, at the very same time as acknowledging the avowed, partial falsehood of the whole endeavour. Note too that in others' hands, even with this self-reflexivity, conjectural history can remain a problematically conservative, partisan genre. This is because it necessarily posits clear lines of development leading, seemingly inevitably, to the writer's present social mode. That present-day social reality is effectively configured as the inevitable, cumulative result of natural processes, as if no other way of life were possible. Dunbar's additional caveat, however, that the conjectural mode's linearity is only heuristic, undoes this tendency, and renders the past even more complexly unknowable than in Rousseau's *Discours*, for example, despite the latter's overt caveats. To approach Dunbar's stadial categories as if they were factual claims about what happened in the distant human past would be fundamentally misguided, therefore. Instead, the reader of the *Essays* must recognize the non-reality, and the very careful epistemology, of the whole intellectual exercise.

In case the political and ideological implications of this careful epistemology were too implicit, Dunbar immediately introduces what becomes one of the

Essays' main preoccupations, the extent to which problems of ideological bias and projection inflect and shape human knowledge. Not only have 'certain appearances in the civil æra' commonly 'been transferred, in imagination, to all preceding times' (*Essays*, p. 6), but 'the same propensity' in the human mind 'which gives life to inanimate objects', has also added 'embellishments of fiction' to our knowledge of both the animal kingdom and the early development of human society (*Essays*, p. 11). The social and political mores of commercial society are similarly described as colouring perceptions of the past: 'In these days of envy, and of interest, we are little able to conceive' the 'force' of the first social bonds of love and affection (*Essays*, p. 25). Both Hume and Smith stress the centrality of falsely inferring intention and agency to human mental life; and Smith especially considers the issue of ideological bias to colour conceptions of human difference. Dunbar, however, might be said to make this latter issue more central to his thought in the *Essays* than is the case in Smith's writing. Dunbar is certainly much more direct than Smith on this issue.

Such emphasis reaches a crescendo in the fourth and fifth of the *Essays*, 'Of the Criterion of Civilized Manners' and 'Of the rank of Nations, and the Revolutions of Fortune'. In accordance with the subtle epistemology we have seen him establish, Dunbar, in these essays, picks apart the 'epithets *barbarous* and *civilised*', which apparently 'occur so frequently in conversation and in books' (*Essays*, p. 141). The strategy which achieves this thorough and extended deconstruction is to make the same distinction Dunbar's Scottish peers emphasize, between lay knowledge and more dispassionate, epistemologically sophisticated reasoning:

> The opinions of the vulgar suggested by instinctive propensities, not formed by reasoning, always ascribe to the progress of science and of art, wherever they have once apprehended the idea of this progress, a superiority of the most decisive kind, in all that is fortunate and desirable in the lot of man. But speculative reasoners are not wholly agreed on this head. (*Essays*, p. 148)

Here then, the claim that quotidian judgements are propelled by 'instinctive' mental propensities builds on the Humean, foundational sceptical distinction between natural, unthinking passions and tendencies on the one hand, and deliberate, abstracted reasoning, or philosophy, on the other. This is a distinction that Smith's thought also works with and extends across his whole career. We should note here too that the opposite mode to this lay conception of knowledge is that of 'speculative reasoners'. What this means, in other words, is that the most sophisticated and carefully considered version of human thinking is not to be understood as the solid grasping of material reality, or of real, evidenced factuality. Instead, human thought at its highest level of development is actually 'speculation'. Like 'conjecture', this self-reflexive term denotes claims and assertions that themselves acknowledge their vexed, limited, and partial nature. Speculations are in this sense complex surmises that contend for their plausibility, but that at the same time make their actual status (as mostly untethered from an unknowable reality) and actual function (as informed but not certain claims) totally transparent. Ferguson, for instance, is careful to configure his own, passionately held assertions, in his *Essay on the History of Civil Society*, of 1767, as 'notions [...] entertain[ed] [...] in speculation', but as perhaps not 'entirely fruitless to mankind', and as therefore a 'pardonable' form of well-intentioned vanity.[38]

For Dunbar, the phenomenon of prevailing, problematic notions of barbarism and civilization is significantly magnified by the human tendency towards hubris. The 'common acceptation' of these terms, he tells us, 'supposes that the difference between one nation and another may be prodigiously great', 'that some happy and distinguished tribes of men are, in all respects, generous, liberal, refined, and humane', 'while others, from their hard fate, or their perverseness, remain in all respects illiberal, mischievous, and rude' (*Essays*, pp. 145–6). Such thought is grossly simplistic, in other words, lumping together seemingly related qualities and assuming a sharp line of distinction between one state and the other. Partisan hubris, nationalism and narrow, unthinking pride are the drivers of this common judgement, for Dunbar. But, as he circles around and returns again and again to this set of issues, in the *Essays*, it is consistently clear that his analysis of these phenomena is Humean and sceptical, because it is diagnosing an inevitable and unavoidable orientation in human quotidian thinking, rather than censuring a local or alterable cultural phenomenon. Thus, following on from the previous quotation sketching the totalizing form in which 'civilization' is normally approached, Dunbar performs a significantly broader reframing of this issue:

> This general supposition with regard to the condition of human nature, is implied in that opinion of their own superiority over other nations which Europeans are prone to entertain: a superiority which, like that assumed by the Greeks, the Romans, and the Chinese, is supposed by those who claim it to be absolute and immense; yet, if brought to the standard of virtue and felicity, it may appear very inconsiderable in respect of the populous Asiatic nations, who have flourished long under extensive monarchies, and not very great in respect even of the simplest and rudest race of men inhabiting the frozen shores of Greenland, or placed beneath the fervour of a vertical sun, along the Guinea coast, or on the Banks of the Orinoco. (*Essays*, pp. 146–7)

---

[38] Ferguson, *Essay*, p. 209.

At first here then such cultural hubris is a modern 'European' phenomenon. But it is immediately revealed to pertain to both the Classical 'Greeks' and 'Romans', as well as to the 'Chinese'. Dunbar's points, very clearly, are that this sense of 'superiority' is extremely widespread, is so common as to be almost unremarkable, but also that it is effectively illusory. One cannot simply assign cultural success to one people, or mode of being; and the size or cultural reach of a society cannot be considered an indication of its 'virtue' or 'felicity'. It is for this reason that Dunbar enumerates the qualities that are most conventionally associated with 'civilization'. His list includes '[w]arm and steady affections', 'fidelity to engagements' and 'laws', 'sciences' and 'fine arts' (*Essays*, p. 143). (He notably glosses 'commercial arts' as 'almost of an indifferent nature' (*Essays*, p. 144)). But Dunbar uses this enumeration to note that 'no nation has ever possessed' all these qualities 'in their highest excellence, nor has any subsisted as a people (short periods of convulsion and anarchy excepted) without a very considerable degree of one or more of those which are to be accounted most essential' (*Essays*, p. 145). When probed in detail, in other words, the epithet 'civilized' quickly seems more like interested prejudice than insightful analysis.

The ideological solution Dunbar arrives at, in order to suggest how a practice of prejudiced superstition could be rethought along more accurate and judicious lines, is one modified from a repeat claim amongst earlier Scottish and French sceptics. This is the 'system of nature' claim: human systems of thought may be inevitably limited and incorrect, given what Hume terms the 'strange infirmities' of the 'human understanding';[39] but despite this, the natural world can be thought of as actually functioning as a coherent and interconnected 'system', even if human observers can only glimpse aspects of these workings. Smith, in this vein of thought, announces both his *Theory of Moral Sentiments* of 1759 and later *Wealth of Nations* as attempts to describe the 'system of nature' in human moral and social matters (this is an exercise that involves critiquing other extant systems as limited by the dynamics of human comprehension, and self-reflexively highlighting how he himself is caught in the same epistemological impasse).[40] Dunbar's analysis of cultural difference makes the following, closely related claim:

---

[39] Hume, *Enquiries Concerning Human Understanding and Concerning the Principles of Morals*, p. 120.

[40] See Smith, *Theory*, p. 292 and Smith, *Wealth of Nations*, II: 687. Jean-Baptiste le Rond d'Alembert's parallel claim is made in the 'Discours Préliminaire' to the *Encyclopédie*: 'The universe, if we may be permitted to say so, would only be one fact and one great truth for whoever knew how to embrace it from a single point of view' ('Preliminary Discourse')

> It ought to be supposed that, if other nations were as far inferior to us, as we are willing to imagine, their condition would evidently tend to decay and extermination. With regard to the inferior orders of being, both animal and vegetable, it seems to be a law of nature, that, wherever they cannot attain, in some very considerable degree, the honours, if I may so speak, and the emoluments of their existence, there they gradually decline, and at last cease to exist at all. Is man an exception from the general law? or may it not rather be believed, that, wherever any tribes of mankind subsist, and do not manifestly decay and hasten to extermination, there, though appearances belie it, they must have attained a measure of worth and of felicity not much inferior to that which the most admired nations have actually attained? (*Essays*, pp. 147–8)

Dunbar's recourse to both the 'animal and vegetable' 'orders of being', like his reframing of the question of cultural prejudice beyond Europe and beyond the present, serves to invoke a bigger perspective from which to consider what is 'natural', even in human matters. Dugald Stewart's 1794 analysis of conjectural history draws attention to this gesture (using Smith as his example) as the ultimate end of this genre of knowledge. For Stewart, conjectural history turns its readers' attention away from false, supernatural explanations for human phenomena, and away from a focus on individual statesmanship, to the 'general provision which nature has made for' humankind.[41] We might note that Stewart himself is actually taking up a position on the vexed question of social development, here, for his full statement refers to the 'general provision' for 'the improvement of the race'.[42] In Dunbar's hands, however, 'improvement' has been thoroughly cast into doubt already by his opening remarks on linearity. Here in this 'animal and vegetable' passage, consequently, Dunbar's image is notably plural and open, promoting different human social modes as parallel to a globally varied inventory of flora and fauna, each of which represents successful growth, development and survival. This version of the contemporary 'system of nature' claim is thus clearly very far removed from a hierarchy of different modes of being with so-called civilization at its apex, or indeed from a proto-racialized set of judgements on different peoples' capacities and tendencies. Likewise it stands at a considerable distance from the claim that is commonly inferred from contemporary stadial history – Smith's would be the prime example – that social difference across the early modern globe should be understood as different positions on the chronological one-way route towards progress. We should note, in this passage, finally, that the epistemological and rhetorical logic through which Dunbar makes these

---

[41] Stewart, *Account of the Life and Writings of Adam Smith, L. L. D.*, pp. 403–78 (455).
[42] Ibid.

points never allows for simplistic false certainty. The phrases '[i]t ought to be supposed' and 'it seems to be a law of nature' render the whole issue one of how one frames one's inquiry into social difference, of what appears logical from one's avowedly limited perspective, and indeed of what the consequences are of certain ideological positions. The key argumentative intervention – 'may it not rather be believed . . . ?' – likewise makes an appeal to logical plausibility, given a germane and nuanced marshalling of the wider context, rather than asserting anything that could be described as certainty or factuality.

This passage thus stands at the heart of Dunbar's analysis of social difference, in his *Essays*. But it is by no means the end of his careful intervention into contemporary thinking. For Dunbar in fact uses this platform of epistemological sophistication and breadth as the basis for establishing a direct moral perspective on the global politics of his day. Once again, this methodology is entirely in line with the thought of his contemporaries, and with the widely shared political ideology that has its roots in sceptical analysis. But Dunbar's particular handling of these issues generates an idiosyncratic stance. In order to see this aspect of Dunbar's thought, we must note, first, that the *Essays* allow that the contemporary degeneration thesis might refer, in a likely limited and simplistic form, to a genuine feature of large-scale social change. Noting the scattered evidence of now-deserted human settlements and constructions across North America, Dunbar asserts that it 'may [. . .] be inferred [. . .] that there are large chasms in the annals of many countries; and that we have obtained but an imperfect acquaintance with the fortune of governments, and the vicissitudes of the species' (*Essays*, p. 186). Invoking the same evidence of the limited human senses with regard to the Earth's motion that Smith uses, Dunbar thus notes that the 'rise and decline of nations' are 'liable to be confounded', and that 'apparent motion may be as different from the real, in the political as in the natural world' (*Essays*, p. 186). Again stressing the consistently limited human knowledge of social change, Dunbar also notes that attempts to explain such transformations have likely been grossly exaggerated. Referring to the contemporary theory of 'climate', and its '[m]echanical and local causes', for instance, Dunbar contends that because these 'so visibly predominate', 'the imagination invests' them 'with a dominion that reaches the very essence of our frame' (*Essays*, p. 155). This is another of the many habits of mind reinforcing cultural hubris, for Dunbar. His next two sentences thus read: 'Hence the mutual contempt of nations. Hence the rank which Europe, at this day, usurps over all the communities of mankind' (*Essays*, p. 155).

Through this observation, Dunbar lays considerable emphasis on opposing this specifically European manifestation of cultural hubris, grounded and justified in this instance by the theory of climate. While the details of European activity in the Americas cause him, in a later essay, to recoil from their description – 'the pen drops from my hand, in reciting the enormities acted by Europeans in the new hemisphere' (*Essays*, p. 396) – here, in this analysis of cultural hubris itself, the patterns of thought behind such activities lead to an extended attack on their implicit logic:

> [Europe] affects to move in another orbit from the rest of the species. She is even offended with the idea of a common descent; and rather than acknowledge her ancestors to have been co-ordinate only to other races of Barbarians, and in parallel circumstances, she breaks the unity of the system, and, by imagining specific differences among men, precludes or abrogates their common claims.
>
> According to this theory, the oppression or extermination of a meaner race, will no longer be so shocking to humanity. Their distresses will not call upon us so loudly for relief. And public morality, and the laws of nations, will be confined to a few regions peopled with this more exalted species of mankind. (*Essays*, pp. 155–6)

Dunbar's analysis of contemporary European cultural superiority indicates that the logics pertaining to later so-called scientific racism are largely anticipated in contemporary culture. The idea that the 'law of nations' only fully applies to the 'few regions peopled with' the 'more exalted species of mankind', for example, invokes countless examples of intercultural brutality, right up to the present. Extending the intellectual dangers of 'theory' – and its falsely neat assertions – into the realm of global politics, Dunbar here thus configures European cultural superiority, together with its attendant 'oppressions' and 'exterminations' of supposedly 'meaner race[s]', as an instance of widespread, erroneous and highly problematic thinking. Such assumptions are thus described, referring back to the 'law of nature' governing 'animal and vegetable' life, as 'break[ing] the unity of the system'. Likewise they 'abrogate', unjustifiably, the in-fact solid 'claims' common to all mankind. For Dunbar, moreover, the modern European manifestation of this false thinking represents the 'utmost extent' of an always problematic 'theory' of cultural superiority that is nevertheless 'of high antiquity' (*Essays*, p. 158). On this point, Dunbar alludes to Ferguson's assertion that this 'propensity [. . .] is the most remarkable in the whole description of mankind' (*Essays*, p. 158). Again, in other words, a clear line of demarcation is drawn between the false and problematic patterns of 'instinctive', quotidian thinking and the more subtle logics of self-reflexive 'speculation'. The former should be seen to shape the world as it stands. The latter strives, by means of applying its subtle epistemology to political matters, to disillusion its readers from their instinctive bias.

Dunbar's political intervention in this mode should not be thought of as simply a counter-ideology to nascent colonialism, however. Instead, in common with Smith's moral and political thought, Dunbar's sceptical analysis of the glimpses it is possible to make of the 'system of nature' recognizes the ultimately wider benefit even of erroneous quotidian judgements. After listing further examples of '[n]ational vanity' as it applies to those from Greece, Labrador, China, Congo, and several American and African 'tribes', Dunbar thus notes that '[s]uch partiality, when not carried into an extreme, answers a noble end', that of ensuring peoples' satisfaction amongst their 'local circumstances' and 'established forms' (*Essays*, pp. 159–60). In this manner, in common with his peers' sceptical analyses of the paradoxes of the human condition, Dunbar is not in any sense claiming that such cultural hubris could cease. But nevertheless, a rounded and informed moral position might be arrived at in spite of such ongoing 'instinctive propensities'. So while 'the illusions of vanity, and the insolence of pride' seem to be 'most inherent to nations and to ages intoxicated with prosperity and affluence' (*Essays*, p. 168), 'commerce' itself, if practised on slightly more informed terms, might still offer the prospect of something approaching global equality and respect:

> Commerce, the boast of modern policy, by enlarging the sphere of observation and experience, promised to undeceive the world, and to diffuse more liberal and equal sentiments through the several parts of an extended system. But commerce, it is to be feared, has, in some instances, been productive of the very contrary effects; and by exposing, if I may say so, the nakedness of society, and uniting, in one prospect, its most distant extremes, has heightened the insolence of nations, and rendered their original and natural equality, to a superficial observer, more incredible. (*Essays*, p. 168)

By placing different modes of social life in close proximity and contact with one another, commerce has, 'in some instances', aggravated the false vanity of cultural superiority and 'heightened the insolence of nations'. But this force also still offers the prospect of 'diffus[ing] more liberal and equal sentiments' across the globe. This stance, we should note, is closely connected to that Smith takes up in the *Wealth of Nations*: 'nothing seems more likely to establish [...] equality of force', between European and other states, 'than that mutual communication of knowledge and of all sorts of improvements which an extensive commerce from all countries to all countries naturally, or rather necessarily, carries along with it'.[43]

---

[43] Smith, *Wealth of Nations*, II: 626–27. See also Dunbar, *Essays*, p. 297, where he alludes to Smith's handling of these issues in the *Wealth of Nations*, and pp. 294–95, where he replicates Smith's stance on *laissez faire*: 'In the progress of arts, the local advantages of mankind all over the globe seem to approach nearer to an equality. There arise more incentives to rouze [*sic*] the industry of

Overall though, Dunbar's *Essays* do not simplistically – or progressively – side with a morally informed mode of commerce. As in Smith, while there is a strand in such thinking that makes it seem as if modern commercial society simply needs tinkering with, through informed legislation, to undo its deleterious effects, the bigger intervention being made – by both thinkers – is a casting of subtle but total doubt over the whole logic of, and hierarchy implicit in, 'civilization'. This is why Book V of the *Wealth of Nations* opens up the exact issues of human freedom in non-commercial society we saw Smith stress in the *Lectures on Jurisprudence*. And this is why Dunbar returns, after this moment, to his deconstruction of the term 'civilization', and to his enumeration of the qualities that should be part of this concept, in order to contrast modern European societies with their geographically and chronologically distant alternatives. In this mode, Dunbar first notes that if one was to measure different social modes by their 'riches', 'population', 'antiquity of arts' and 'stability and duration of civil government', it would be 'the Chinese, and the Indians, who must be placed at the head of the species' (*Essays*, p. 189). But since these are the components of what he has already defined as an unthinking, lay-conception of civilization, Dunbar then reminds his reader that, if one follows his own more detailed analysis, 'many an obscure people have possessed [civility] in a degree of perfection which the proudest nations in Asia, or in Europe, could not boast in the days of their splendor' [*sic*] (*Essays*, p. 190).[44] This judgement, notably, once again undoes the chronological logic of conventionally conceived 'progress'. And in this same vein, Dunbar then observes that, contrary to quotidian judgements, 'it is no paradox to affirm, that the court of Fingal was as highly civilized as the court of Lewis XIV [*sic*]' (*Essays*, p. 190). Fingal is the epic hero from James Macpherson's Ossian poetry we will turn to at the end of this study. Dunbar qualifies this assertion with the caveat that he is assuming, in this remark, that 'the picture of manners delineated in a performance, which is now read and admired in almost all the languages of Europe, is a faithful copy of an

---

nations. And a passage being opened in every country for the collective treasures of the earth, general competition and demand secure emoluments and rewards to every people, more accurately proportioned to the measure of active exertions, and the wisdom by which they are directed. Riches or poverty must no longer be estimated by the position of a people on the globe. Art, if I may say so, alters the dispensation of nature, and maintains a sort of distributive justice in the division of opulence among mankind. Such at least would be the tendency of things, if all restrictions on trade were abolished by a concert among nations, calculated for the common benefit of all. But mutual jealousies derange and encumber their mutual efforts.'

[44] Note that I am not claiming that such 'lay-conceptions' are misreadings of more sophisticated philosophy. On the contrary, I am using as a heuristic device the distinction that contemporary scepticism makes between 'instinctive propensities' or everyday prejudice, on the one hand, and more deliberately reasoned and philosophically informed thinking, on the other.

original' (*Essays*, p. 190). Such phrasing might be said to refer to the accuracy of Macpherson's translations, rather than, or as much as, the authenticity of the whole enterprise. Either way, the role of the works of Ossian in undermining the quotidian conception of civilization is nevertheless significant for Dunbar, who explains it at length. In outline first, in the court of Fingal, 'the arts were totally unknown'; in that of Louis XIV, 'they were at the height of their splendor' (*Essays*, p. 191). Then, deploying his own more sophisticated terminology of civilization, Dunbar probes this comparison further:

> But the want of those graces which the arts confer, was more than compensated at the one court, by virtues in which the other was deficient. And if fidelity, generosity, true dignity of mind, are preferable to disingenuity, perfidy, servile adulation; if the former qualities are to be numbered among polite accomplishments, and the latter to be placed in the opposite column, who would not prefer the civilization of Fingal's court to that of the other, though embellished by all arts and sciences? (*Essays*, p. 191)

This passage again renders the process of making judgements on matters of human social difference one standing at a considerable remove from certainty or factuality. Thus it is a careful and provisional rhetorical question that makes Dunbar's intervention: 'if' the moral contrast the passage is making seems sound, then 'who would not prefer' the social realm of early Scotland to that of seventeenth- and eighteenth-century France?

Dunbar's next sentence reminds his reader, even more directly, that his stance is one of sceptical suspended judgement. For he clarifies that he is not 'presuming [...] to decide the dubious pretensions of mankind' (*Essays*, p. 191). We are, in these matters, far removed from certainties, therefore, and deep into doubtful, but nevertheless still valuable, assertions. Because Dunbar's nuanced methodology has been thoroughly explained by this point, in other words, the political energies of his analysis are clear. Lay conceptions of both 'civilization' and 'progress' are comprehensively undermined, by Dunbar's examination of them, and a more epistemologically and morally subtle mode of thinking is suggested. Dunbar's reader must recognize, however, that this more subtle pattern of thought is not one that simply counters one body of evidence with another. Instead, two competing epistemologies are set out and contrasted, by the *Essays*. On the one hand, there is lay knowledge, with its 'instinctive propensities' and its unreasoned, notably self-flattering, judgements. On the other, there is careful marshalling of a more complex field of surmise and estimation. The latter, it is clear, thus proceeds not by factuality or certainty, but by a sophisticated and subtle inquiry always attentive to the limits of human knowledge. Moreover, these limits seem to pertain especially, in Dunbar's handling, to the field of sociocultural difference as it seems to have existed across human history.

Overall, therefore, it would be inappropriate and highly reductive to denominate Dunbar either a 'primitivist' or an advocate of progress. Such a label would ignore the wholesale epistemological and political complexity through which contemporary thought – in this mode – handles the issues of social difference and wide-scale historical change, rendering a highly subtle set of dynamics a simplistic matter of opinion. For Dunbar's thought, as it occurs in the *Essays*, represents a snapshot of the epistemological rigour and sophistication through which mid to late eighteenth-century thought often addresses social difference across time, and across the globe. As his regular allusions to contemporary thought evidence, his analysis does not stand alone, in other words, but is in conversation with an intellectual culture, especially in Scotland, that considers fundamental matters of epistemology to be of structural importance for both human self-comprehension and for political consciousness. Thus while one may be tempted to isolate eighteenth-century Aberdeen as possessing an intellectual culture particularly conducive to progressive ideas, such as Abolitionist sentiment, in contrast to the climate of Edinburgh and Glasgow, the present analysis evidences, rather, that participation in the reigning sceptical epistemology in fact engenders very closely related political stances. This is why Dunbar's *Essays* express such precise affinity with and Smith's writing on the intercultural possibilities of global trade, for instance. As we turn away from Dunbar now, to the thought of John Millar, we will still be within the orbit of this set of sceptical assumptions. But we will also see isolated and problematic departures from such epistemological orthodoxy, back towards the lay model of knowledge Dunbar sketches.

2 John Millar and the Certainties of Colonialism

John Millar's *The Origin of the Distinction of Ranks*, of 1771, is in many ways an orthodox 'natural history', as we have explored the logic of that mode so far. Millar's text, indeed, uses this generic categorization to announce its intellectual enterprise, and Millar's own central status within Scottish-Enlightenment culture – he was Professor of Civil Law at the University of Glasgow from 1761, as well as a close friend of Adam Smith's and intellectual disciple of both Smith and of David Hume – might make this adherence to Scotland's reigning methodological orthodoxy unsurprising. But the reason that Millar exemplifies, in my analysis, a second position on the epistemological spectrum of contemporary progress-discussions is that the *Distinction of Ranks* is modified, across its three editions, in such a way as to become – in its final, 1781 edition – notably unmoored from the dominant sceptical postures of 'modesty' and 'doubt', as Millar's contemporaries express these. Moreover, the more straightforwardly certain – and politically dogmatic – elements that Millar adds in to his text are not only presented as if the issue of ideological bias does not apply to them. They also stand very close to the political stance that his close contemporaries – like Dunbar – consider the exemplification of such bias. In this final form that the *Distinction of Ranks* takes, furthermore, these notably certain, proto-colonialist claims hold an uneasy relationship with the still-extant, more varied and less certain details of Millar's own analysis. Millar's texts becomes, in other words, notably uneven and contradictory, therefore, in such a way as to move it away from the more epistemologically rigorous analysis of his academic contemporaries.

By assessing Millar's thought in terms of the precise epistemological and political positions he takes up, in relation to those of his contemporaries, my analysis also works against the critical consensus that Millar is simply an advocate for progress. Anna Plassart, as one representative example, has recently summed up this stance by contending that Hume, Smith, Adam Ferguson, William Robertson and Millar are 'all united in the belief that England had achieved a state of political and civil liberty such as to give it an exceptional situation amongst the large states of modern Europe'. Furthermore, for Plassart, these figures 'therefore sought to offer "scientific" and historically sophisticated explanations for this exceptional state of liberty'.[45] The claim that these figures advocate progress, which I have countered for Hume and Smith elsewhere, might be said to apply less problematically to Millar, given his statements in the final edition of the *Ranks*. Even this judgement would have to ignore the original form of Millar's text, however, as well as the ongoing contradictions it espouses in its final form. The point of my analysis is to demonstrate that the often simultaneously multiple stances contemporary texts generate in relation to questions of progress are better thought of as consequences of the nature of socio-historical knowledge itself in the mid eighteenth century, rather than as an individual author's belief, not least because Millar's 1781 text is thoroughly contradictory on this issue. Plassart's other claim, that these mid to late century analyses are 'scientific' is also problematic, from the perspective of the present study. This is because, like Clifford Siskin's claims considered earlier, it suggests a smooth continuity between Scottish-Enlightenment thought and the later, nineteenth-century development of the so-called scientific method (itself a much more complex and contradictory phenomenon than the term 'scientific' now implies). The

---

[45] Plassart, 'Scientific Whigs?', 93–114 (95–96).

recent identification of the dominance of scepticism in Scottish-Enlightenment thought, by contrast, illuminates how Hume's famous 'science of man' is in fact one based on, and tracing the ramifications of, the radical limitations of human knowledge, not a budding empiricist confidence in observable data. Scottish-Enlightenment philosophy thus performs a shared consideration of the 'strange infirmities of the human understanding' insofar as that sceptical metaphysics underpin and inform its intellectual and intercultural stances, up until at least the early 1780s.

While modern readers are most likely to encounter Millar's 1781 text first then, this being the core text presented in Aaron Garrett's 2006 scholarly edition, let us turn instead to the 1771 first edition, so as to see Millar's more orthodox account of natural history. For, as Garrett puts it, Millar 'drastically rewrote his introduction [...] for the third edition'.[46] In 1771, then, Millar opens his 'Preface' – anticipating Dugald Stewart's later explanation and defence of the conjectural form – by surveying the limited functions of human inquiries into social history. These fall into just two areas, for Millar. First –

> By observing the systems of law established in different parts of the world, and by remarking the consequences with which they are attended, men have endeavoured to reap advantage from the experience of others, and to make a selection of those institutions and modes of government which appear most worthy of being adopted.[47]

Millar's term 'endeavoured' here is a subtle marker, which Smith also deploys repeatedly in the *Wealth of Nations*, that such a task may not be fully achievable. It anticipates the direct cautionary proviso Millar is about to make. Millar's second function for social history is also expressed with a similar subtlety, and one might say with a growing sense of caution: 'To investigate the causes of different usages, hath also been esteemed a useful as well as an entertaining speculation' (*Ranks*, p. 284). In this sentence then, such histories are classed as 'speculations', the contemporary term, as we saw with Dunbar, for subtle, conjectural reasonings that acknowledge their limited and largely non-evidentiary basis. Here, further, Millar also points towards these problems of epistemological limitations with his phrasing that such 'investigat[ions]' have been 'esteemed [...] useful', as if this might be an overblown judgement of their practitioners. Again, this is a self-reflexive commonplace in contemporary sceptical philosophy. The idea that such 'speculations' might be 'entertaining' – which is again encompassed by the seeming estimation of their authors – is another subtle indicator, in the context

---

[46] Garrett, 'Millar's Preface to the First Edition', p. 284.
[47] Millar, *The Origin of the Distinction of Ranks*, p. 284 (hereafter cited parenthetically as *Ranks*).

of the reigning sceptical proto-psychology, that human knowledge cannot be considered a certain grasping of a knowable realm of material reality.

In his next paragraph, Millar reiterates the contemporary distrust of 'abstracted [...] theories', promoting instead – following Hume and Smith as well as Diderot and d'Alembert – 'real experiments' (*Ranks*, p. 285). This last term alludes to Isaac Newton's apparent distrust of 'hypotheses' in his *Principia*, of 1729, and his consequent emphasis on experimental deduction. In the wake of Hume's deployment of the term 'experiment' in the *Treatise*, also by allusion to Newton, it comes to include any reasoning based on observations on real life, or second-hand reports of these, as opposed to non-observational reasoning. This moment of methodological meta-commentary is consequently also the occasion for Millar to express at some length the issue of the traps of evidence, and the problems of false certainty, that contemporary scepticism emphasizes:

> In perusing such records, however, the utmost caution is necessary; and we must carefully attend to the circumstances in which they were framed, in order to ascertain the evidence which they afford, or to discern the conclusions that may be drawn from them. As the regulations of every country may have their peculiar advantages, so they are commonly tinctured with all the prejudices and erroneous judgments of the inhabitants. It is therefore by a comparison only of the ideas and the practice of different nations, that we can arrive at the knowledge of those rules of conduct, which, independent of all positive institutions, are consistent with propriety, and agreeable to the sense of justice. (*Ranks*, p. 285)

Not only is 'the utmost caution' required, by the philosopher of human society, in this account. Because human judgements are inseparable from 'prejudices and erroneous judgements', the philosopher-historian must also perform the informed and subtle process of 'comparison' – involving 'carefully attend[ing] to the circumstances in which' each account of the past was 'framed', as well as deliberating over the extent to which each record 'affords' 'evidence' – in order to generate 'knowledge'. Such knowledge, moreover, we should note, is not simply factual and certain, but is contingent: it is 'consistent with propriety' and 'agreeable to the sense of justice'. Millar is therefore here giving his own idiosyncratic expression of the tenets of contemporary scepticism, in which that mode's proto-psychology and savviness with regard to false certainty must inform the philosopher's carefully provisional and subtle 'speculations'. Indeed, Millar's next point is that modesty and caution can be the only outcomes of such inquiries: 'When these enquiries are properly conducted, they have [...] a tendency to restrain that wanton spirit of innovation which men are apt to indulge in their political reasonings' (*Ranks*, p. 285). Political reasoning, the logic of this statement implies, is notably looser and less careful than philosophical reasoning. And because, for Millar, the latter teaches doubt and non-intervention – he uses a 'machine' metaphor to caution against naively 'produc[ing] the utmost disorder and confusion' (*Ranks*, p. 285) – its parameters should be recognized to approximate the logic of *laissez faire* that Ferguson had expressed four years before this publication, and that Smith would restate five years later. For both Ferguson and Smith, leaving alone, politically, is the only philosophically consistent position, because of the severe limitations on human knowledge contemporary scepticism pinpoints.

All these elements of Millar's epistemological meta-commentary come together, therefore in this 1771 text, in his closely following statement that the *Ranks* is a 'natural history':

> The following observations are intended to illustrate the natural history of mankind in several important articles. This is attempted, by pointing out the more common and obvious improvements in the state of society, and by showing the influence of these upon the manners, the laws, and the government of a people. (*Ranks*, pp. 285–6)

The term 'natural history', then, as Millar positions it, incorporates all the epistemological nuances he has just set out, as well as the 'utmost caution' against using it as the basis for false certainty and falsely simplistic politics. The phrasing of this quotation is also notably careful with the issue of the status of such a history. Millar's observations aim to 'illustrate' his natural, conjectural history, rather than state it, in its full, monolithic entirety. Furthermore, Millar's 'attempt' to compose such material is to be thought of as synonymous with 'pointing out the more common and obvious improvements in the state of society'. The majority of information will be too detailed, too intricate and too rare to be visible, comprehensible or recordable, in this formulation. Hume had described sceptical intellectual inquiry, in a connected manner, as needing to acknowledge that there are very often countless 'principles too fine and minute for [...] comprehension'.[48] Millar's natural history in the *Ranks*, in other words, should be thought of, even with the subtle methodological meta-knowledge he carefully expresses, as only a superficial and simplistic grasping of an in-fact unmanageable complexity. The latter, in this orthodox sceptical view, will always remain inaccessible to the human contemplator.

Millar's epistemological framing to his inquiry is sceptically orthodox therefore, restating the tenets and logics that pertain to natural history as his philosophical contemporaries also understand these. And what this stance leads to, in the body of Millar's text itself, is a mode of analysis alive to the contradictions

---

[48] Hume, *Treatise*, p. 438.

within apparent social evolution. The opening of his first chapter, 'Of the Rank and Condition of Women in Different Ages', encapsulates this well. Following the core, Smithian, economic stadial categories, for instance, Millar speculates that the 'savage who earns his food by hunting and fishing, or by gathering the spontaneous fruits of the earth' (*Ranks*, p. 93), while intellectually and socially limited in a sense, is actually 'peculiarly distinguished' by the ease with which he can 'gratify' his sexual 'appetites' (*Ranks*, p. 94). This is because 'there are no differences of rank to interrupt the free intercourse of the sexes' (*Ranks*, p. 94): 'The members of different families, being all nearly upon a level, maintain the most familiar intercourse with one another, and, when impelled by natural instinct, give way to their mutual desires without hesitation or reluctance' (*Ranks*, p. 94). This supposition of libidinal 'liberty' in pre-civilization, moreover, engenders a vexed, partly Rousseauvian portrait of the anxieties and contradictions pertaining to commercial modernity. Millar thus contrasts his imagined 'savage' with his modern – also male – counterpart as follows:

> [The savage] arrives at the end of his wishes, before they have sufficiently occupied his thoughts, or engaged him in those delightful anticipations of happiness which the imagination is apt to display in the most flattering colours. He is a stranger to that long continued solicitude, those alternate hopes and fears, which agitate and torment the lover, and which, by awakening the sensibility, while they relax the vigour of his mind, render his prevailing inclinations more irresistible. (*Ranks*, p. 94)

Here, then, Millar's analysis might be said to complicate – in a related manner to Smith's observations in the *Lectures on Jurisprudence* – the simplistic notion that progress from so-called savagery to commercial society is a positive process of amelioration. Passages like this – and there are many in Millar's analysis – also hold an uneasy relationship with Plassart's assertion that Millar is espousing the exceptional state of 'civil liberty' to be found in contemporary England. This is because the apparent sophistications of social and psychic life in modernity are here also configured as 'agitat[ions]' and 'torment[s]'. 'Sensibility', therefore – the vogue for which is at its height in the early 1770s – is configured as both a gift of intense mental experiences *and* a fallen state of moral 'torment' that stands at a considerable remove from the savage's immediate libidinal satisfactions. The latter 'arrives at the end of his wishes' almost without contemplation. These claims, therefore, stand close to – and arguably add further detail to – Rousseau's (also conjectural) assertion that the 'immoderate transports of every passion, fatigue, exhaustion of mind, the innumerable sorrows and anxieties that people in all classes suffer, and by which the human soul is constantly tormented' are all 'the fatal proofs that most of our ills are of our own making'.[49] To be sure, in Rousseau's scheme, it is the apparently 'solitary' 'state of nature' that is to be contrasted with modern mental degeneracy. This is not the same as the Scottish hunter-gatherer supposition Millar is using. But nevertheless, the political energies of the two, in these examples, are closely related. This is why, indeed, moving the same issue away from simply libidinal freedom, that Millar goes on to summarize that '[r]ude nations are usually distinguished by greater freedom and plainness of behaviour, according as they are farther removed from luxury and intemperance' (*Ranks*, p. 105). Note again, contrary to the idea of modernity providing the acme of liberty, that 'freedom of behaviour' is the main focus of this contrast.

As Millar's account of social development takes in further stages beyond hunter-gatherer 'savagery', it is notable that the apparently vexed status of psychic life in commercial modernity remains a repeat preoccupation. In his consideration of agricultural society, for example, Millar uses 'the compositions of Ossian' as a primary body of evidence (*Ranks*, p. 126). And whereas Dunbar – later – includes a proviso concerning the accuracy of Macpherson's translations, Millar displays no such doubt or reticence. For Millar, then, what the Ossian poetry embodies and expresses is 'a degree of tenderness and delicacy of sentiment which can hardly be equalled in the most refined productions of a civilized age' (*Ranks*, p. 126). Even the intellectual and emotional sophistications that Millar previously expressed as the hallmark of modernity actually occur in the eras before the commercial present, in other words. And again, for Millar, this is evidence bolstering a broadly Rousseauvian judgement. This is why Millar uses the same phrase as Rousseau to describe the apparently ideal, middle stages of social development: the 'golden age'. Immediately after a lengthy quotation from Macpherson's 'The Battle of Lora, a Poem', that is, Millar's analysis of the significance of *Ossian* is as follows:

> In the agreeable pictures of the *golden age*, handed down from remote antiquity, we may discover the opinion that was generally entertained of the situation and manners of shepherds. [...] There is good reason to believe, that these representations of the pastoral life were not inconsistent with the real condition of shepherds, and that the poets, who were the first historians, have only embellished the traditions of early times. [...] This refinement was the more likely to become the subject of exaggeration and poetical embellishment; as, from a view of the progressive improvements in society, it was contrasted, on the one hand, with the barbarous manners of mere savages; and, on the other, with the opposite style of behaviour in polished nations,

---

[49] Rousseau, *Inequality*, p. 84.

> who, being constantly engaged in the pursuit of gain, and immersed in the cares of business, have contracted habits of industry, avarice, and selfishness. (*Ranks*, p. 128)

Ossian's portrait of early, agricultural society, then, is to be considered representative of an apparently widespread conception of that mode of social life. It encapsulates 'the opinion that was generally entertained of the situation and manners of shepherds'. Further, this conception is not to be considered inaccurate, for Millar, it being also compatible with such peoples' 'real condition'. The historical evidence contained in the poetry of Ossian, therefore, once again throws an unfavourable light on commercial modernity. While savages may be 'barbarous', in terms of manners, the inhabitants of 'polished nations' are 'immersed in the cares of business' to such an extent that their mores must be expressed as though they were unfortunate diseases: they 'have contracted habits of industry, avarice, and selfishness'. To configure 'industry' as a problematic moral 'habit', here, is clearly in line with Dunbar's distrust of the 'commercial arts', and with Ferguson and Smith's critical lines of analysis concerning commercial mental stultification. It also continues to put the details of Millar's conjectures in tension with his adopted stadial scheme which, in overview at least, moves apparently forwards, from savagery to commercial modernity. It demonstrates, indeed, that in 1771 at least, that stadial scheme is primarily a heuristic device, held only lightly in Millar's analysis, so as to explore the more vexed and complex details of social difference.

This complex intellectual stance is why Millar's analysis is open to the logic of the contemporary degeneration thesis that Spadafora refers to. In his section considering 'The effects of great opulence, and the culture of the elegant arts, upon the relative condition of the sexes', for instance, Millar addresses the limitations of commercial progress:

> It should seem, however, that there are certain limits beyond which it is impossible to push the real improvements arising from wealth and opulence. In a simple age, the free intercourse of the sexes is attended with no bad consequences; but in opulent and luxurious nations, it gives rise to licentious and dissolute manners, inconsistent with good order, and with the general interest of society. The love of pleasure, when carried to excess, is apt to weaken and destroy those passions which it endeavours to gratify, and to pervert those appetites which nature has bestowed upon mankind for the most beneficial purposes. The natural tendency, therefore, of great luxury and dissipation is to diminish the rank and dignity of the women, by preventing all refinement in their connection with the other sex, and rendering them only subservient to the purposes of animal enjoyment. (*Ranks*, pp. 151–2)

While the focus of this set of observations remains the role of sexual appetites in social life, Millar's claims follow the logic of many contemporary degeneration claims. The forces of opulence and luxury unleash a moral dissipation which might be considered to turn a 'civilized' society to a downward trajectory in terms of moral refinement. This is suggested to be a 'natural tendency', the isolation of which, for Millar as for Dunbar and others, is the primary function of conjectural, natural history – as Dugald Stewart later confirms. But, as is the case with many contemporary expressions of this sort, Millar is careful to express something of the epistemological subtlety that governs this claim, and not allow it to be understood as a matter of simplistic certainty or belief. His formulation 'It should seem [...] that there are certain limits ... ' configures his claim as one of plausible appearance following subtle marshalling of complex and inconclusive evidence. Again, it would be a mistake, in this epistemological context, to consider this statement as a matter of belief or of certainty, or as a quasi-factual claim about the events of human social history.

It is in the context of these orthodox epistemological subtleties that it is possible to see how Millar's modifications to the introduction to his *Ranks*, for the final, 1781, third edition, tip the balance of energies in his text slightly further towards a politically dogmatic model of certainty. Millar's 1781 'Introduction' does still express the same epistemological caveats as his 1771 'Preface' – that inquiries such as his are 'speculations' with limited aims, for example, or that the uncertain evidence for such inquiries needs to be handled with caution. But the new 'Introduction' mutes the significance of these sceptical observations by placing them alongside a confidently expressed and seemingly totalizing account of human social progression. The effect of this juxtaposition is to render the caveats only applicable to relatively small-scale matters of how one explains phenomena, as if human comprehension of the grand sweep of progress towards civilization is in need of no such self-reflexivity.

The 1781 depiction of social progression thus begins with an extremely bold judgement on human difference as it is visible across the eighteenth-century globe:

> When we survey the present state of the globe, we find that, in many parts of it, the inhabitants are so destitute of culture, as to appear little above the condition of brute animals; and when we peruse the remote history of polished nations, we have seldom any difficulty in tracing them to a state of the same rudeness and barbarism. (*Ranks*, p. 84)

The language of the first sentence of this quotation is notably extreme, in the context of Scottish-Enlightenment thinking about social difference. As Millar's 'Introduction' comes five years after the publication of the *Wealth of Nations*, one might contrast his stance with Smith's there. When Smith strategically opens up the problem of social difference in Book V of that work, he does so at the same time as signalling his distrust of stadial categories. He uses the phrase 'barbarous societies', but immediately glosses it with the caveat 'as they are called'.[50] Moreover, the point Smith is making at this moment is that other social modes, as they have been witnessed around the globe – by the same bodies of evidence that Millar is using – actually generate more sophisticated citizens, in mental and physical terms, than commercial modernity. For Smith, in those societies, 'every man [...] is a warrior', and – whereas citizens of commercial modernity are benumbed in mental and moral terms, – '[e]very man too', in so-called barbarous societies, 'is in some measure a statesman'.[51] Smith's analysis might also be said to be representative of the epistemologically orthodox stance on such issues, as Dunbar and Ferguson's analysis demonstrates. Millar, however, while seemingly highly aware of this context, takes a different route through these same issues. For him, a 'survey' of the 'present state of the globe' reveals the 'inhabitants' in 'many parts of it' to be 'so destitute of culture, as to appear little above the condition of brute animals'. To describe the citizens of 'many' other societies as barely human in this manner is thus to take up the same stance that Dunbar classified as the dangerously biased quotidian logic impelling European atrocities around the globe. Millar's second, closely connected sentence, moreover, asserts that the community of which he is a part – presumably modern Britain, or modern Europe, given the context ('we' can hardly mean 'speculative philosophers' given the stark difference in stances just noted) – 'have seldom any difficulty' in locating the same borderline inhumanity in the ancestors of the present-day 'polished nations' themselves. This two-part observation thus combines an assertion that there is no epistemological issue with making these claims, with the total judgement that non-civilized peoples live 'little above the condition of brute animals'. In this manner, Millar here adopts a political, moral *and* epistemological stance in stark contrast with the thought of his contemporaries – despite the still-remaining overall consanguinity between his 'natural history' in the *Ranks* and the also-conjectural, stadial analyses of his peers. Observations such as this one in the 'Introduction' also now stand at odds with the remarks that remain in the body of his text, such as those concerning the '*golden age*' Ossian apparently truthfully depicts. The poetry of Ossian, as we will see Macpherson and Hugh Blair explain presently, is consistently presented as depicting present-day Scots' 'ancient' ancestors.

Millar's additional, 1781 tour through the historical periods of social difference these sentences introduce thus takes the economic stages Smith had

---

[50] Smith, *Wealth of Nations*, II, 783.   [51] Ibid.

coined, but expresses their features, and indeed their existence, as something much closer to certainty than we have encountered in this study so far. While some of Millar's statements deploy the language of presumed certainty conjectural history requires, because they have been introduced by the problematic political certainties we have just explored, such phrasing functions more immediately as a continuation of those certainties than as a series of speculations and surmises within acknowledged limits. Millar's account of 'savage' life is a case in point:

> A nation of savages, who feel the want of almost every thing requisite for the support of life, must have their attention directed to a small number of objects, to the acquisition of food and clothing, or the procuring shelter from the inclemencies of the weather; and their ideas and feelings, in conformity to their situation, must, of course, be narrow and contracted. (*Ranks*, p. 84)

Again, we can get a clear sense of the ramifications and nature of Millar's position by contrasting it with contemporary equivalents. Here, then, is Ferguson's 1767 account of what contemporary proto-anthropological 'description' of the 'naked savage' has actually found:

> Who would, from mere conjecture, suppose, that the naked savage would be a coxcomb and a gamester? that he would be proud or vain, without the distinctions of title and fortune? and that his principal care would be to adorn his person, and to find an amusement? Even if it could be supposed that he would thus share in our vices, [...] yet no one would be so bold as to affirm, that he would likewise, in any instance, excel us in talents and virtues; that he would have a penetration, a force of imagination and elocution, an ardour of mind, an affection and courage, which the arts, the discipline, and the policy of few nations would be able to improve. Yet these particulars are a part in the description which is delivered by those who have had opportunities of seeing mankind in their rudest condition; and beyond the reach of such testimony, we can neither safely take, nor pretend to give, information on the subject.[52]

Another example, this time from after Millar's text, would be Samuel Hearne's travel narrative recounting his experiences with the native-American tribes in what is now southern Canada, *A Journey From Prince of Wales's Fort in Hudson's Bay to the Northern Ocean*. Hearne published this work in 1795, but the experiences it recounts took place between 1769 and 1772. One relevant instance of Hearne's analysis is his lengthy description of the culinary mores of the 'Northern Indians'. These are, at first, disgusting to European observers, he records, but then, when these same Europeans – including Hearne himself – overcome their

---

[52] Ferguson, *Essay*, p. 76.

'prejudice', they 'readily agree' in 'pronouncing them the greatest dainties that can be eaten'. As this pattern is repeated across many aspects of these tribes' ways of living, moreover, Hearne records that '[i]n fact, it is almost become a proverb in the Northern settlements, that whoever wishes to know what is good, must live with the Indians'.[53]

So while contemporary discourse is frequently open to the many sophistications of so-called savage life, in the years around Millar's text, Millar's 1781 account of the stages of social progress depicts that same mode of life as intellectually and sentimentally cramped in the extreme: 'their ideas and feelings, in conformity to their situation, must, of course, be narrow and contracted'.[54] Note here that the normally conjectural, knowingly speculative phrase 'must be' is here interrupted by the interjection 'of course' so as to render it an emphatic assertion of certainty following on from Millar's seemingly certain statements about the near-animality of 'many' humans. 'Savage' life, for Millar, is thus one marked by lack and by want, to such an extent that its members are again barely alive: they 'feel the want of almost every thing requisite for the support of life'. It is worth noting that this position, which, in the context of recent criticism concerning stadial history, can seem to be an unremarkable commonplace, is actually at odds with Smith's most influential handling of this issue. Smith's *Lectures on Jurisprudence* had in fact stated – in both student reports – that subsistence was always an easy matter, even in 'savage' life – specifying how this is the case for food, for clothing and for lodging, which all seem to require just the unassisted and easy labour of a solitary individual.[55] He had also included this judgement in the *Theory of Moral Sentiments*, in 1759 (even making this same point more emphatically in his 1790 emendations to that text) and then taken up the same position in the *Wealth of Nations*.[56] This context again allows us to see that, while Millar

---

[53] Hearne, *A Journey from Prince of Wales's Fort in Hudson's Bay to the Northern Ocean*, p. 318.

[54] It would of course be possible to bring in parallel evidence from other contemporary travel narratives. Broadly these also work as evidence of how contemporary texts frequently both consider non-European peoples inferior (almost always by invoking the part-stadial terms 'savage' and 'barbarous') *and* record those peoples' many freedoms and positive qualities in comparison with European modes of living. Hearne's text certainly follows this pattern. I will address this pattern of contradiction directly in this Element's 'Conclusion'. My point here is that Millar's 1781 claims are very clear overstatements in the context of exactly this repeat-tension, because of their emphasis on how 'narrow and contracted' 'savage' life is.

[55] See Smith, 'Report of 1762–3', p. 335. Smith's larger point is that what are in one sense 'frivolous' aesthetic distinctions 'lead [...] men into customs with regard to food, clothing, and lodging which have no relation to convenience and are often contrary to the ends proposed to be supplied by those things'. Life is easy, in other words, but the human drive towards beauty and refinement 'give in the pursuit more distress and uneasiness to mankind' than is in any way necessary (pp. 336–37).

[56] See Smith, *Theory*, p. 213, a 1790 addition to the text which states that human subsistence is, in all geographical contexts, 'very easily supplied'. In 1759, the *Theory* nevertheless follows the

overall might be considered an intellectual disciple of Hume and Smith, his 1781 'Introduction' to the *Ranks* moves his analysis into very different political territory from the thought of those two philosophers.

Millar's account of social progress continues, in 1781, in the same vein as these comments, continuing to tell the stadial story of 'savage' hunter-gathering leading towards 'cultivating the ground' (*Ranks*, p. 84), the 'establish[ment]' of 'property' (apparently 'the great source of distinction among individuals') (*Ranks*, p. 85), and then the 'complex [...] government' of 'an opulent community' (*Ranks*, p. 85). This whole account forms one long paragraph, and is in this manner truncated so as not to allow any epistemological or evidentiary issues to arise in its narration. It also presents, by its smooth rhetoric, a portrait of social progress as inevitable, as highly logical, and indeed as ultimately unremarkable. This, for example, is Millar's account of how agricultural life leads, gradually and smoothly, in to commerce:

> According as men have been successful in these great improvements ['of cultivating the ground'], and find less difficulty in the attainment of bare necessaries, their prospects are gradually enlarged, their appetites and desires are more and more awakened and called forth in pursuit of the several conveniencies of life; and the various branches of manufacture, together with commerce, its inseparable attendant, and with science and literature, the natural offspring of ease and affluence, are introduced, and brought to maturity. (*Ranks*, p. 84)

The regular pacing of Millar's prose embodies his claim, here and throughout this 1781 paragraph, that these developments are each 'the natural offspring' of what has come before. In the suggestions that 'appetites and desires' are 'awakened and called forth', and that 'science and literature' are 'brought to maturity', for instance, it is the language of naturalistic change and development that Millar uses. The effect of this is – again in stark contrast to parallel claims by Dunbar, Smith or Ferguson – to depict human social development as a one-way, always-occurring, cumulative and natural process.

As we have seen exemplified in Dunbar's thought, the repeated, sceptical observation that works against the human desire for certainty is that concerning

---

Lectures on Jurisprudence on this issue, stating, for instance that '[i]n what constitutes the real happiness of human life, [those without property] are in no respect inferior to those who would seem so much above them. In ease of body and peace of mind, all the different ranks of life are nearly upon a level, and the beggar, who suns himself by the side of the highway, possesses that security which kings are fighting for' (p. 185). This is also one of the points of Smith's extended parable of the poor man's son in this work. In the *Wealth of Nations*, ease of subsistence is stated repeatedly. See I: 162–63, I: 178 and I: 237. Smith also notes, in support of this claim, that it seems only to be 'in civilized society' that there is a 'scantiness' of 'subsistence' among 'the inferior ranks of people' (WN, I: 97).

the ideological bias – and the hubris – that inheres in all human thought. From Hume onwards, Scottish-Enlightenment thinkers demonstrate the totality of their self-surveillance on this issue by repeatedly casting sophisticated, self-conscious doubts over their own 'speculations'. Millar, by contrast, must be seen to represent a different epistemological case, and must be seen to occupy – in 1781 at least – a second position on the epistemological spectrum of contemporary progress narratives, if Dunbar's writing represents a first. This is because, in 1781, Millar's 'Introduction' still expresses the conventional sceptical caveats, but does so in a manner that does not interfere with the seeming certainties of his newly added stadial scheme. Thus, following this defiantly expressed paragraph concerning the stages of history, Millar's next preoccupations are all about the doubts of historical enquiry. Every one of these expressions of epistemological doubt, however, applies to a more limited case of problematic argumentation that does not dislodge the certainty of Millar's stadial scheme in the slightest. In this vein he expresses doubts about the logic of the founding-statesman myth that many societies evidence (*Ranks*, p. 86), doubts regarding the repeatedly 'fabulous histor[ies]' of early society (*Ranks*, p. 87), and doubts regarding contemporary 'climate' theory (*Ranks*, p. 87–9). All these brief sketches are summaries of conventional, contemporary sceptical deconstructions. On 'climate' theory, for example, Millar's point stresses both the status of such claims as 'conjectures', and the difficulty of assessing these with anything approaching certainty: 'How far these conjectures have any real foundation, it seems difficult to determine' (*Ranks*, p. 89). But in all these cases, such conventionally sceptical argumentation is allowed to operate on only a limited terrain, never casting its doubts over the whole enterprise of stadial history itself. Millar's nine paragraphs on these epistemological issues then lead to him denominating his text a 'natural history' (*Ranks*, p. 89), using the same sentences as in 1771 indeed. The effect, however, is very different, because his 1781 additions stand as if isolated from the epistemological nuances he explores.

This problematic effect is bolstered even further, in 1781, moreover. Both the 1771 'Preface' and the 1781 'Introduction' end with the same paragraph concerning the difficulty of ascertaining and isolating historical facts. Thus, 'the reader, who is conversant in history, will readily perceive the difficulty of obtaining proper materials for speculations of this nature' (*Ranks*, p. 90). After outlining these difficulties in conventionally sceptical terms, Millar suggests that if 'extraordinary facts' are corroborated by very different reports, then they can be credited (*Ranks*, p. 90). Further, if such coincidence of evidence aligns with 'reason[ing]' regarding 'those particular customs', 'the evidence becomes as complete as the nature of the thing will admit' (*Ranks*, p. 90). Finally, in this chain of reasoning, Millar summarizes that in this case, '[w]e cannot refuse our assent to such evidence, without falling into a degree of scepticism by which the credibility of all historical testimony would be in a great measure destroyed' (*Ranks*, p. 90). This set of statements clearly carves out a method of achieving something approaching evidenced certainty in the face of sceptical analysis – all the while acknowledging the value of the sceptical worries over evidence. (It approximates, indeed, what Matytsin records as the recourse to probability that occurs frequently, for similar reasons, in contemporary French intellectual culture.) But in 1771, as the 'Preface' does not include a dominating, seemingly certain overview of the shape of human history, such caveats serve to cast the light of epistemological subtlety and caution over everything one is about to read. One ought to be sceptical regarding all historical evidence, and any consideration of the human past is a very difficult enterprise, epistemologically speaking – so these comments imply, in 1771. There are limited certainties, in cases where the motley body of evidence can be carefully parsed. But the mixed and complex analysis to follow (which still follows in 1781 of course) confirms the difficulty of the enterprise. In 1781, by contrast, because of the unchallenged and notably certain stadial account that Millar has added in, such comments now refer backwards, as it were, towards that powerfully expressed, monolithic account of the necessary and natural shape of human progress. Now, in 1781, Millar's text reads as if even sophisticated sceptics do not 'refuse' their 'assent' to the 'historical testimony' that stands behind the stages of history as Millar has expressed them. The climate of contemporary philosophy may be subtly and comprehensively sceptical, it is now implied, but the 'we' of which Millar is a part is here implied to be those same sceptics who nevertheless consider the four-stage, one-way shape of human history to be sufficiently evidenced.

The political stance which frames and summarizes Millar's *Ranks*, in 1781, is thus notably distinct from the 'suspended judgement' on intercultural matters that characterizes the texts of his fully sceptical academic peers. Millar's confident stadial claims, moreover, are consonant with both the proto-racialized narrative of European superiority that Dunbar pinpoints and with the later, early nineteenth-century colonialist claims concerning how non-European peoples can be helped towards social, cultural and economic progress. Millar's additional 1781 claims include the idea that 'the similarity of' human 'wants, as well as the faculties by which those wants are supplied' means that the social movement of progress is one in which people's 'appetites and desires are more and more awakened and called forth in pursuit of the several conveniencies of life' (*Ranks*, p. 84). This claim forms the basis of the nineteenth-century political-economic commonplace that, in David Ricardo's terms, 'the remedy for the evils' under which non-civilized peoples suffer, is to 'create new wants, and to implant new tastes'.[57] This is because such desires are considered, in this line of thought, to impel social progress towards systems of private property, commercial exchange and the network of institutions that attend on and underpin these systems in European societies. And, of course, behind the seemingly technical and analytical language Ricardo – and Millar – use on this issue, there stands a long and disturbing history of the forced imposition of European institutions and patterns of behaviour on peoples all around the globe. Dunbar's *Essays* published just a year before Millar's final text comprehensively illustrate contemporary knowledge of such issues, as does Smith's slightly earlier *Wealth of Nations*.

Millar's *Origin of the Distinction of Ranks* is thus to be considered epistemologically and politically contradictory on the disputes and concerns attendant on contemporary progress-discussions, in its final form. For even in 1781, Millar's more nuanced analysis in the body of his text remains, including on the 'golden age' that agricultural life represents, and on the moral and psychic degeneracy commercial society seems to bring with it. Millar's use of *Ossian* is especially striking because, as we shall see now, James Macpherson, Ossian's putative translator, actually asserts – repeatedly – that such poetry comes from the 'earliest' period of human society. The name of Ossian becomes synonymous with a set of culturally primitivist claims, in the 1760s, in other words. Millar's deployment of it alongside a stridently ameliorative logic of progress is thus notably jarring, when placed alongside Macpherson's own account of the poems.

3 Ossian and the Biases of Commercial Modernity

James Macpherson's Ossian project – comprising *Fragments of Ancient Poetry Collected in the Highlands of Scotland* (1760), *Fingal: An Ancient Epic Poem in Six Books* (1761), *Temora: An Ancient Epic Poem in Eight Books* (1763) and the collected *Works of Ossian, the Son of Fingal, in Two Volumes* (1765) – is not normally considered alongside contemporary stadial history. The 'coherent critical perspective' that has emerged in the last few decades, according to Dafydd Moore, nevertheless recognizes that the poems function as complex gambits in contemporary political debates.[58] For Moore, this 'sophisticated', collective critical view thus

---

[57] Ricardo, *Principles*, I, 100, n. 1; a similar idea is expressed (in a more subtle way) in John Stuart Mill's connected analysis in his 1848 *Principles of Political Economy*, I, 12.

[58] Moore, 'Heroic Incoherence in James Macpherson's *The Poems of Ossian*', 43–59 (43).

suggests that *Ossian* was in large part generated as a response to the fact that 'the language of virtue in the eighteenth century was still tied to the essentially civic and masculine realm of the active and patriotic warrior-citizen' and that 'on the face of it this language had little in common with the emerging discourse of passion, benevolence, and humanity'.

Thus, '*Ossian* suggested that society did not have to choose between "strength and bravery" and "courtesy and sentiment", but could combine both within a system of what we might call civic sensibility'.[59] This perspective is undoubtedly insightful, accessing as it does the extent to which the Ossian poems consistently emphasize a mode of being, in their protagonists and narrator, holding much in common both with the contemporary practice of sensibility and with a classical-republican model of martial virtue. As Moore notes, this stance works well to 'explain the fascination exerted by *Ossian* over some of the greatest literary and philosophical minds of the age'.[60]

By placing the Ossian project alongside the stadial histories of James Dunbar and John Millar, however, the present analysis aims to make visible a different side of the Ossian project. This is its engagement with, and contribution to, the argumentative terrain of contemporary stadial history. For Dunbar's reference to the court of Fingal, and Millar's reference to the 'golden age' Ossian depicts, both demonstrate that Ossian's poetry is important, and indeed privileged, evidence in contemporary stadial history. Alongside the clear contemporary importance of Ossian *for* contemporary stadial history, though, the original scholarly headnotes and 'dissertations' published alongside the Ossian poems, penned by Macpherson himself and also by his collaborator and mentor Hugh Blair, actually function *as* versions of conjectural histories in their own right. Both Macpherson and Blair, for example, use the poems as powerful evidence from which to suggest their own – differing – stages through which human history might pass. And the commentary of both figures also unpicks, at length, the apparent lessons the poetry teaches concerning social difference and its modifications through time (all with a particular eye to situating modern Scotland in relation to wider European culture). These tasks not only belong to the genre of knowledge that is conjectural history; they are also carried out, by both Macpherson and Blair, alongside frequent reference to the same subtle sceptical epistemology that we have seen inform Dunbar's and Millar's thought, and that stands behind many other contemporary Scottish analyses of social development and difference. When approached with detailed knowledge of contemporary stadial history and its sophisticated methodology, therefore, the writings of the Ossian project can be seen to represent a third position on the

---

[59] Ibid., pp. 43–44.   [60] Ibid., p. 43.

epistemological spectrum of contemporary progress narratives. For while Macpherson and Blair allude to the severe limitations on human knowledge the sceptical tradition describes, they also configure the poetry of Ossian – by virtue of its widely experienced dramatic power and immediacy – as providing a shortcut towards something much closer to certainty than the 'suspended judgement' conjectural history's conventional evidence provides. Poetry, in other words, is configured by the Ossian project as outranking the other forms of cultural and historical evidence available in the mid eighteenth century. This is a claim of some importance for contemporary culture. It is also another highly probable explanation for the sensational popularity of, and the fascination around, the Ossian poetry.

From Macpherson's first published translations of 'ancient', 'highland' poetry, then, the Ossian project is announced in reference to contemporary considerations of social development. The 1760 'Preface' to the *Fragments of Ancient Poetry*, which Richard B. Sher asserts is written by Blair,[61] thus claims that the poems of the volume 'abound with those ideas, and paint those manners, that belong to the most early state of society'.[62] While the more formalized Scottish stadial categories are yet to be constructed, in 1760, this phrasing – 'the most early state' – nevertheless refers to the widespread contemporary vogue for interpreting global cultural difference as stages of progress. David Hume had performed (avowedly provisional) conjectural history of this sort in the final book of his *Treatise of Human Nature* (1739–40), and had considered human society in terms of economic stages (again in a highly conditional form) in his *Essays*, published between 1741 and 1752. Jean-Jacques Rousseau's *Discourse on Inequality* functioned in comparable terms, in 1755, and followed on from the sketch of conjectural history penned by Jean-Baptiste le Rond d'Alembert in the 'Discours Préliminaire' (of 1751) to his and Denis Diderot's *Encyclopédie* (1751–72). And these works represent just a few of the manifestations in formal philosophy of a widespread cultural vogue, especially in France and Scotland, for thinking of this sort. Macpherson and Blair's other key signpost, in this first Ossian publication, and other anticipation of the political ramifications of this project, is that the highland poetry being presented in translation represents a particularly pure and uncorrupted body of evidence through which to access this 'early' social mode. The 'succession' of family 'Bards' in northern Scotland, the 'Preface' claims, generated a 'tradition' comprising this poetry. And 'tradition, in a country so free of intermixture with foreigners, and among a people so strongly attached to the memory of their ancestors, has preserved many of them in a great measure

---

[61] Sher, 'Blair, Hugh'.
[62] Macpherson, *Fragments of Ancient Poetry Collected in the Highlands of Scotland and Translated from the Galic or Erse Language*, p. iii (hereafter cited parenthetically as *Fragments*).

incorrupted [*sic*] to this day' (*Fragments*, p. vi). Note here then that this poetry is to be thought of as containing a particularly privileged form of cultural knowledge, thanks to its unusual purity. Because the highlands have been 'so free of intermixture with foreigners', Macpherson's translations – it is implied – cut through the complexities and intercultural contaminations of other cultural sources to offer an unmediated experience of 'early' society. In other words, the very same issue of the unavailability of solid evidence of human pre-history which Dunbar and Millar summarize, and which Hume and Rousseau equally highlight, configures Macpherson's translations as a form of pre-historic Holy Grail. They – supposedly – cut through the unknowability of the past by transporting their readers right back to prehistory.

Macpherson's (or Blair's) statements here, in this first Ossian publication, should thus be understood to allude, in a multi-faceted form, to the problems of knowledge contemporary culture finds pertaining to questions of social development.[63] Even in this relatively brief and limited form, they are at once proto-racialized signposts of the supposed original dignity and purity of Scottish culture *and* an announcement that the vexed issue of social development has been made significantly clearer, thanks to the unmediated and real access to the past the poems provide. (This issue of mediation is why the 'Preface' repeatedly stresses that Macpherson's 'translation is extremely literal', 'even' imitating 'the arrangement of the words in the original' (*Fragments*, p. vi).) It is this same cluster of claims that Macpherson expands on, moreover, in his subsequent publications. Both *Fingal* in 1761 and *Temora* in 1763 contain not just prefaces restating these same ideas, but also 'dissertations' written by Macpherson formalizing even further the sociopolitical insights provided by the poems. In 1761 then, Macpherson reads the doubts of some of his contemporaries over the authenticity of the poems as an instance of what the prevailing sceptical proto-psychology describes as the ideological bias implicit in quotidian judgements. Claiming to have spoken with a sceptic concerning the veracity of *Fingal*, who was then convinced of the poem's authenticity after reading it, Macpherson explains this phenomenon as an effect of the 'prejudices of the present age against the ancient inhabitants of Britain'.[64] The latter, for Macpherson, are commonly 'thought to have been incapable of the generous sentiments to be met with in the poems of Ossian' (*Fingal*, n. p.).

---

[63] I express doubt over this text's authorship because my analysis exposes internal evidence for there being two distinct modes of handling the Ossian claims across the Macpherson and Blair's work. This first 'Preface' thus seems much more in line with Macpherson's later contributions. It might thus be considered Blair writing in the persona of Macpherson.

[64] Macpherson, *Fingal: An Ancient Epic Poem in Six Books*, [n. p.] (hereafter cited parenthetically as *Fingal*).

And this supposed bias leads Macpherson to reflect at some length on the apparently widespread belief in what contemporary discourse terms 'progress' and 'civilization':

> If our [fore]fathers had not so much wealth they had certainly fewer vices than the present age. Their tables, it is true, were not so well provided, neither were their beds so soft as those of modern times; and this in the eyes of men who place their ultimate happiness in those conveniencies [*sic*] of life, gives us a great advantage over them. I shall not enter farther into this subject, but only observe, that the general poverty of a nation has not the same influence, that the indigence of individuals, in an opulent country, has, upon the manners of the community. The idea of meanness, which is now connected with a narrow fortune, had its rise after commerce had thrown too much property into the hands of a few; for the poorer sort, imitating the vices of the rich, were obliged to have recourse to roguery and circumvention, in order to supply their extravagance, so that they were not without reason, reckoned in more than one sense, the worst sort of people. (*Fingal*, n. p.)

It is striking that although *Fingal* is published two years before Adam Smith's first recorded account of the 'division of labour' in his *Lectures on Jurisprudence*, Macpherson here anticipates the parameters and terms of Smith's argument quite closely – albeit that Smith's emphasis is different. 'Conveniencies', manufactured commodities, may be more abundant in modern times than in the past, but this does not mean that the 'manners', virtues or 'sentiments' of the past can be thought of as having undergone an ameliorative process of progress. For both Macpherson and Smith, however, as for Dunbar later, this is nevertheless the unthinking and biased assumption that most people make.

Macpherson's intervention here, building on the wealth of evidence Ossian's writings apparently provide, is thus akin to Dunbar's later position. Lay conceptions of civilization (what contemporary scepticism configures as un-thought-out, instinctive biases) represent a false and partial lumping together of apparently positive human qualities with the commercial arts. But more detailed knowledge of alternative social modes reveals that modern moral categories like 'meanness' cannot be transferred, anachronistically and imprecisely, to whole societies. Instead, the strikingly 'generous sentiments' found in Ossian point towards the many sophistications of human life being distributed across time, as across space. Macpherson is thus deploying the epistemological critique of lay knowledge that has its roots in contemporary scepticism in order to deconstruct and loosen the ideological biases of modernity. He is moving the question of social difference away from a quotidian focus on commodities and 'conveniencies', towards the moral and social qualities that cluster around sensibility, manners and virtues. The effect of this epistemological method, therefore, is – as in Dunbar's thought – to generate a form of cultural relativism that finds conventional narratives of 'progress' to be both limited and falsely flattering to their present-day exponents. But in this instance, it is the evidentiary impetus of Ossian's poetry, rather than a judiciously handled survey of the vexed issue of knowledge of the past, that is driving these gestures. As Macpherson notes, towards the end of *Fingal*'s 'Preface', 'the compositions of Ossian are not less valuable for the light they throw on the ancient state of Scotland and Ireland than they are for their poetical merit' (*Fingal*, n. p.).

In the more formal 'Dissertation concerning the antiquity &c. of the poems of Ossian the Son of Fingal', included before the text of *Fingal* itself, these same political and argumentative energies are transformed even further down the path towards becoming formal conjectural history. Macpherson, for instance, recaps contemporary scepticism's distrust of 'systems' and uses it to configure accurate historical knowledge as a near-impossibility. His statements performing these tasks, moreover, form the opening sentences of this 'Dissertation' in such a manner as to become the formal epistemological framing of his analysis. Macpherson thus recreates the exact same epistemologically sophisticated essay form that Hume had developed in the previous decade. The effect of all this is to generate a warning, for Macpherson's readers, of the extreme difficulty of isolating real historical knowledge:

> Inquiries into the antiquities of nations afford more pleasure than any real advantage to mankind. The ingenious may form systems of history on probabilities and a few facts; but at a great distance of time, their accounts must be vague and uncertain. The infancy of states and kingdoms is as destitute of great events, as of the means of transmitting them to posterity. The arts of polished life, by which alone facts can be preserved with certainty, are the production of a well formed community. [...] The actions of former times are left in obscurity, or magnified by uncertain traditions. Hence it is that we find so much of the marvellous in the origin of every nation; posterity being always ready to believe any thing, however fabulous, that reflects honour on their ancestors. (*Fingal*, p. i)

Four years after this publication, Voltaire would also apply the sceptical deconstruction of lay knowledge to 'history', in his article for the *Encyclopédie* titled by this term, and would also recount how 'the origins of all peoples are absurd'.[65] Macpherson here anticipates many details of Voltaire's analysis, while also attributing the popularity of necessarily false histories to ideological bias. The 'fabulous'

---

[65] Voltaire, 'History', [n. p.].

is rendered believable by its flattering implications, 'reflect[ing] honour' on a people's 'ancestors'. Note here too that 'systems of history' are 'vague and uncertain' and should be considered closer to entertainment – 'afford[ing] [...] pleasure' – than to useful information. This is again a parallel statement to the contemporary sceptical deconstruction of systematic knowledge, anticipating – for instance – the anonymous 1765 *Encyclopédie* article on 'System', which notes that systems are often 'artistic masterpieces' that are simultaneously 'admirable' and 'the most extravagant sort of folly'.[66]

This sceptical framing to the *Fingal* 'Dissertation' is used, by Macpherson, as a platform on which to construct a history of early Scotland's place in the developmental story of European societies. But it would be something of a stretch to call this particular strand of the Ossian project a 'conjectural' or 'natural' history, because Macpherson in fact uses a rhetoric of factual certainty, rather than that form's 'presumed certainty'. Hume had already, in the *Treatise* and his *Essays*, shown how conjectural history could be performed self-reflexively, with not only careful adherence to the language of presumed certainty, but also frequent moments of meta-commentary making the precise epistemological status of his claims as transparent as possible. Macpherson's epistemological framing to the *Fingal* 'Dissertation' demonstrates knowledge of these materials, indeed. Adam Ferguson, a few years after *Fingal*, in 1767, also pens his *Essay on the History of Civil Society* in such a way as to ensure that almost every sentence includes reference to the vexed nature of historical knowledge. But ultimately the *Fingal* 'Dissertation' alludes to the terms and beliefs of the current sceptical orthodoxy in such a way as to cast the light of epistemological rigour over its actually more quotidian claims. Thus, the crux of the historical claims Macpherson makes is that, first, the 'Celtic nations' were 'once the masters of Europe from the mouth of the river Oby, in Russia, to Cape Finisterre, the western point of Gallicia in Spain' (*Fingal*, p. ii); and second, following on from this, that the present-day Irish are descended from the Scots and not the other way round, because '[s]ome adventurers passing over from those parts of Britain that are within sight of Ireland, were the founders of the Irish nation' (*Fingal*, p. iii). Note then, first, that these statements are made with a sense of simplistic certainty absent from the full epistemological rigour we followed in Dunbar, and that is also to be found, before Macpherson, in Hume and Smith's writing. Secondly, note that, for all Macpherson's reference to the modern biases that favour flattering histories here, the historical narrative that the Ossian poetry is said to produce, is itself notably flattering to present-day Scots. Indeed, rhetorically and strategically, the self-reflexive allusion to the

---

[66] Anon., 'System', [n. p.].

problems of ideological bias Macpherson makes should be understood to shore up, and to provide seemingly sophisticated cover for, his own flattering history. The *Fingal* 'Dissertation' is thus deploying the tenets of contemporary sceptical moral philosophy in order to give inflated credence to its own lay-conception of cultural history. We should note too that in this manner Macpherson is also amplifying the suggestion made in the original, shorter 'Preface' to the *Fragments of Ancient Poetry*, that the poems of Ossian contain evidence of the proto-racial purity and pre-eminence of the Scots themselves.

Macpherson's next, 1763 'Dissertation' preceding *Temora* represents the closest Macpherson himself gets to producing a genuine conjectural history founded on the Ossian materials. Blair's *Critical Dissertation on the Poems of Ossian, Son of Fingal*, meanwhile, also published in 1763, with its more rigorous scholarly methodology, could be thought of generating a new generic development from that form. The *Temora* 'Dissertation' first – the full title of which is simply 'A Dissertation' – maintains the Humean essay form Macpherson had deployed before *Fingal* by opening with a sense of epistemological rigour:

> Nations, small in their beginnings and slow in their progress to maturity, cannot, with any degree of certainty, be traced to their source. The first historians, in every country, are, therefore, obscure and unsatisfactory. Swayed by a national partiality, natural to mankind, they adopted uncertain legends and ill-fancied fictions, when they served to strengthen a favourite system, or to throw lustre on the ancient state of their country.[67]

Again, then, knowledge of the past is falsely inflected by 'national partiality' and comprises 'uncertain legends and ill-fancied fictions'. But once again such rigour serves to frame the apparently special case of the highland Scots, the evidence of whom remains pure because of the particular geography of their home:

> If tradition could be depended upon, it is only among a people, from all time, free of intermixture with foreigners. We are to look for these among the mountains and inaccessible parts of a country: places, on account of their barrenness, uninviting to an enemy, or whose natural strength enabled the natives to repel invasions. Such are the inhabitants of the mountains of Scotland. (*Temora*, p. ii)

Even though historical knowledge cannot normally be thought of as a mode of 'certainty', then, the case of highland Scotland is different. There, oral

---

[67] Macpherson, *Temora, An Ancient Epic Poem in Eight Books*, p. I (hereafter cited parenthetically as *Temora*).

reporting, normally liable to corruption or bias, is a 'tradition' that can be 'depended upon'.

Here in 1763, as in his 1761 text, Macpherson observes that the particular form of proto-racialized, cultural 'purity' the highland Scots represent also includes their freedom from the problems of commercial modernity. These statements again could be described as giving further credence to Macpherson's analysis, because they run parallel to observations in the fully sceptical versions of intercultural analysis, like those in Smith's lectures, that isolate what seem to be the ideological norms attendant on a social system built around trade:

> As they lived in a country only fit for pasture, they were free of that toil and business, which engross the attention of a commercial people. Their amusement consisted in hearing or repeating their songs and traditions, and these intirely [sic] turned on the antiquity of their nation, and the exploits of their forefathers. (*Temora*, p. ii)

In 1761, Macpherson had similarly stated that 'the introduction of trade and manufactures' to the highlands 'destroyed that leisure, which was formerly dedicated to hearing and repeating the poems of ancient times' (*Fingal*, p. xv). Extending the logic of this claim even further, he had also configured the reading of Ossian's poetry itself as an act of rebellion against the intellectual narrowness of commercial modernity:

> When property is established, the human mind confines its views to the pleasure it procures. It does not go back to antiquity, or look forward to succeeding ages. The cares of life encrease, and the actions of other times no longer amuse. (*Fingal*, p. xv)

It is worth remarking, here that Macpherson's isolation of the stultification of the modern mind by commerce anticipates the significantly more sustained analysis of this phenomenon by Ferguson in 1767 and then by Smith in 1776. Again, in other words, this demonstrates the consanguinity between Macpherson's epistemologically informed analysis and that of his more sceptically orthodox peers. (It also points towards Ferguson and Smith's claims being in common circulation in contemporary culture.) In this instance, however, the outcome of Macpherson's observation is to configure the poetry of Ossian as a privileged and powerful object with which to throw off that mental 'confinement'. This again encapsulates the Ossian project's distance from the repeat 'modesty' and 'suspended judgement' sceptical analysis generates in its most orthodox mode. Everything in Macpherson's commentary serves to further augment the significance and political power of Ossian's poetry. So while this *Temora* 'Dissertation' continually alludes to the orthodox distrust of evidence contemporary scepticism dictates, it does so in order to show how Ossian represents a trump card in such a predicament.

The reason this *Temora* 'Dissertation' stands closest to genuine conjectural history is because it uses these discussions to generate its own categories for stadial history. Macpherson arrives at this point of his analysis by claiming that there was a particular 'species of heroism' that 'subsisted in the days of Ossian', which began to decay soon after this time (*Temora*, p. xii). This shift then leads to Macpherson asserting the following structure of human social development:

> There are three stages in human society. The first is the result of consanguinity, and the natural affection of the members of a family to one another. The second begins when property is established, and men enter into associations for mutual defence, against the invasions and injustice of neighbours. Mankind submit, in the third, to certain laws and subordinations of government, to which they trust the safety of their persons and property. As the first is formed on nature, so, of course, it is the most disinterested and noble. Men, in the last, have leisure to cultivate the mind, and to restore it, with reflection, to a primæval dignity of sentiment. The middle state is the region of compleat [*sic*] barbarism and ignorance. (*Temora*, p. xii)

This passage is almost exactly contemporary with the earliest record of Smith's stadial categories, which were suggested to his Glasgow students in 1762, and which used means of subsistence as their organizational motif – albeit as more of a heuristic tool than a statement of certainty. It might also be said to build on Rousseau's similarly sceptical sketch of social development. Rousseau's emphasis was not on pinning down exact stages, but overall his *Discourse on Inequality* suggests a pre-linguistic and pre-social 'state of nature', followed by a 'golden mean' of small-scale, artisanal society, and then – eventually – the modern world of commerce, disease and degeneracy. Macpherson's categories, in this context, can be seen to use social ties as their most significant heuristic category, but then also to immediately qualify these with the prevailing mode of morality and ideology each stage supposedly brings with it. Thus 'affection' resulting from 'consanguinity' is followed by 'associations for mutual defence' and then 'subordination' to 'government'. And these three stages also connote first, 'natural', 'disinterested' 'nobility'; second, 'compleat barbarism and ignorance'; and third, 'leisure to cultivate the mind', including to reflect on 'primæval dignity of sentiment'.

Macpherson's version of stadial history notably again seems designed to position Ossian's poetry as of central cultural importance. If mankind is naturally disinterested and noble, then it is only in the first stages of complex sociality that such dignity is obscured and hindered. Further, the trajectory of human life, in this set of claims, is to escape from this predicament by 'cultivating', when possible, the original high-pitch of 'sentiment', and to therefore return, by deliberate action and reflection, to their former dignity. Ossian's poetry, in other words, both embodies the original state of 'natural nobility' and offers the promise to its readers of helping them combine morally sophisticated 'subordination to government' with a recreation of their 'primæval dignity'. To devote one's time to 'cultivating' the mind, and to 'reflecting' on the role of 'sentiment' in human social life, is thus to perform a work of cultural destiny, because the development Macpherson describes is configured both as one-way, and as an ameliorative process of intellectual and spiritual advance. Macpherson's much-stressed, extremely 'literal' strategy of translation is again configured by these claims as of prime importance to the Ossian project, therefore. For the largely unmediated access to society's 'earliest' mode the poems are said to promise, from their first appearance in 1760, would be impossible if they were inflected by the mores of commercial modernity. If, though, one takes Macpherson at his word regarding the provenance of the Ossian poetry, and regarding the 'pure' transmission of the poetry from the time of Ossian to the present, *and* regarding Macpherson's own near invisible imprint as translator, then the poems would indeed corroborate, and render plausible, the particularly primitivist version of stadial logic Macpherson suggests. A modicum of the attractiveness of this set of propositions is made visible by reference to the reception of Ferguson's *Essay* in Scotland a few years later. This is because Ferguson's carefully poised 'speculations' in that work point in a similar political direction, recounting, for instance, how modern, effete Europeans were being forced to relearn their natural nobility by confronting the in-fact more morally, individually and martially sophisticated native tribes in North America. The *Caledonian Mercury*, an Edinburgh newspaper, expressed this as follows: 'Ferguson, taking a route different from his contemporaries, has directed philosophy to the heart: has endeavoured to animate the coldness of modern times with the ardent spirit of antiquity; and, to a mercenary and luxurious age, has lifted up the voice which called the Greeks and Romans to virtue and glory.'[68] The cultural politics of Macpherson's stadial claims clearly work in a closely related manner, while also offering the apparently sensational evidence of the Ossian poetry itself. From the perspective of the present analysis, however, it is possible to see that Macpherson's claims require his readers to take a lot on trust. For the contemporary climate of epistemologically precise and informed doubt regarding the mechanisms underpinning knowledge and certainty act as a spotlight on the jumps in logic, and the

---

[68] The *Caledonian Mercury*, 17 February, 1777, quoted in Finlay, 'Rhetoric and Citizenship in Adam Ferguson's *Essay on the History of Civil Society*', 27–49 (43).

argumentative and evidentiary liberties, at work in the Ossian claims. So powerful is this contemporary climate, it seems, that Macpherson must write on its terms, in all his commentary on Ossian, even if this means highlighting where his materials fall short of the standards that climate requires.

The final iteration of the Ossian project we need to consider is Hugh Blair's *Critical Dissertation on the Poems of Ossian, Son of Fingal*, which was published in the same year as *Temora*, 1763. Blair, of course, may well have contributed to the prose around the Ossian poetry we have already considered. He is also the whole project's instigator and Macpherson's mentor, arranging for the publication of the *Fragments* after learning of Macpherson's translations of Gaelic poetry, and then encouraging Macpherson to continue down this path. But Blair's *Dissertation* also represents a distinct strand of the Ossian project. In contrast to Macpherson's epistemologically hybrid dissertations – alluding to sceptical rigour but also making more quotidian political claims – Blair's *Dissertation* is more academic and in some senses more epistemologically cautious. More significantly, in large part Blair shifts the emphasis of discussion from Macpherson's claims that Ossian represents a special and unique case in the vexed field of historical knowledge, to how aesthetic objects such as 'poems or songs' can be thought of as always capturing cultural mores in a different manner from other historical records. Blair's *Dissertation* is in this sense a seminal text in the history of literary criticism. And we are here in a position to see the formative role that conjectural history, and the contemporary version of sceptical epistemology, play in that mode's eighteenth-century development.

Blair's *Dissertation* begins, then, in the now familiar, Humean mode for an essay concerning the human past, of noting the vexed issue of historical knowledge: 'The beginnings of society, in every country, are involved in fabulous confusion; and though they were not, they would furnish few events worth recording'.[69] But for Blair, this conventional impasse can refocus the attentions of the modern historian. This is because an 'ancient' people's 'poems or songs [. . .] present to us, what is much more valuable than the history of such transactions as a rude age can afford, The history of human imagination and passion' (*Dissertation*, p. 1). Note here that 'imagination and passion' may appear, to modern readers, to denote a small subset of the human mental terrain, as if Blair is embarking on a history of the creative faculties, for example, or of the immaterial longings that dog material culture. In fact, in 1763, these two

---

[69] Blair, *A Critical Dissertation on the Poems of Ossian, the Son of Fingal*, p.1 (hereafter cited parenthetically as *Dissertation*).

terms connote the entirety of human intellectual life. This is because, in the cluster of ideas Hume expresses, and that also informs a large strand of contemporary philosophy and culture, the 'imagination' is the primary human faculty, receiving and handling all sense-data, as well as processing larger-scale, theoretical knowledge. The 'passions', likewise, are the drivers of all human mental, physical and social behaviours, even taking in what is commonly termed (then as now) 'reason'. Hume, for instance, clarifies that what conventional thinking terms 'reason' is actually a host of slow-acting passions, which 'operate' with no 'disorder in the temper'.[70] Blair's phrase, announced with a rhetorical flourish by his capitalization, 'The history of human imagination and passion', is therefore claiming that literary artefacts such as the Ossian poetry represent a powerful encapsulation, and preservation, of previous modes of human mental life in their entirety. Further, mental life is to be understood, in this Humean, sceptical intellectual culture, to encompass every human social phenomenon. This is because the sceptical proto-psychology, which exerts such powerful influence over contemporary thought, asserts that each individual is effectively imprisoned in their own mental processes. These may seem to give people access to the external, physical world, but the revelation of sceptical analysis is that they more properly cloister each mind within its own motley, incomplete and inconclusive array of sensations and concomitant ideas, providing knowledge only by analogy and surmise. The human social and political realms, in this view, are to be understood through the natural, mental mechanisms scepticism makes visible. Blair's announcement of his method for accessing 'The history of human imagination and passion' is therefore significantly grander and more total than it appears to a modern reader.

We should note that this central idea of Blair's *Dissertation* holds – in common with Macpherson's claims – the idea that the seeming impasse in human knowledge of the past might be overcome by particular types of evidence. In this sense, Blair is also fundamentally demurring from the reigning sceptical orthodoxy that is visible elsewhere, in which *all* human knowledge of the past is configured as doubtful surmise, the exact status of which must be carefully laid out. But at the same time the methodology he is announcing here – unlike Macpherson's – continues to pay court to sceptical analysis, by reading his encapsulations of the past in terms compatible with the epistemological orthodoxy of his contemporaries. This is why his itself orthodox use of the terms 'imagination and passion' is followed, in his very next sentence, by the phrase 'the notions and feelings of our fellow-creatures' (*Dissertation*, p. 1), the structural role of which configures these terms as closely connected to the

---

[70] Hume, *Treatise*, p. 437.

previous pairing. Hume's architecture of human thought that opens his *Treatise* had classified all ideas as 'impressions' – stemming from sense-data, desires, passions and emotions – and had distinguished how the mind attached different intensities of belief and immediacy to these. Smith, in his *Theory of Moral Sentiments*, in 1759, had similarly used 'fellow-feeling' as the basis for a sceptical account of the usefully false surmises, and the natural projections, the human mind makes in the social and moral realms. Macpherson's terms thus sit in the same orbit as these claims by summarizing the human mental terrain as a matter of a subtle proto-psychology in which carefully fine-grained distinctions need to be made between mental phenomena – and in which mental phenomena themselves are the most telling markers of a mode of being.

Blair's relationship to epistemologically orthodox contemporary models of social development is also much closer than Macpherson's. Whereas Macpherson's *Temora* 'Dissertation' suggested its own stadial model built on social ties, Blair, writing in the same year as Smith's earliest recorded *Lectures on Jurisprudence*, also deploys what are now thought of as Smith's categories:

> There are four great stages through which men successively pass in the progress of society. The first and earliest is the life of hunters; pasturage succeeds to this, as the ideas of property begin to take root; next, agriculture; and lastly, commerce. (*Dissertation*, p. 16–17)

Blair's support of Smith's position (alternatively, this might be another instance of more of a shared consensus being expressed at the same time by the two figures) does come with important differences, however. As noted earlier, Smith's handling of these ideas, as it is recorded in student notes, includes pretty consistent signposts that the whole framework was a heuristic device. Before the *Lectures* Smith had also expressed in writing – with similar directness to Hume – how the basic abstractions of 'man' and 'human nature' were necessary but ultimately false counters of thought, because each individual mind was so varied, so in flux and so walled-in as to be uncapturable.[71] Smith's later handling of the stadial hypothesis in the *Wealth of Nations*, as

---

[71] Smith, 'History of Ancient Logics and Metaphysics', pp. 118–32 (121): 'When I lay my hand on the table, the tangible species which I feel this moment, though resembling, in the same manner, is numerically different too from that which I felt the moment before. Our sensations, therefore, never properly exist or endure one moment; but, in the very instant of their generation, perish and are annihilated for ever. Nor are the causes of those sensations more permanent. No corporeal substance is ever exactly the same, either in whole or in any assignable part, during two successive moments, but by the perpetual addition of new parts, as well as loss of old ones, is in continual flux and succession. Things of so fleeting a nature can never be the objects of science, or of any steady or permanent judgment. While we look at them, they are changed and gone, and annihilated for ever. [...] Man is perpetually changing every particle of his body; and every thought of his mind is in continual flux and succession.'

we saw in the context of Millar, also signals his distrust of its terms and his part-support for the thesis of the tendency towards degeneration in social mores. In Blair's *Dissertation*, by contrast (as in Macpherson's stadial terms), these 'four great stages' are notably more monolithic, more necessary, as well as distinctly linear and one-way: 'men successively pass' through them, 'in the progress of society'. Strategically, we could say that this reference to Smith, or to something akin to an academic consensus, again sures up and gives credence to Blair's case. Blair is certainly claiming that Ossian fits verifiably into stadial history. His next sentence asserts that '[t]hroughout Ossian's poems, we plainly find ourselves in the first of these periods of society' (*Dissertation*, p. 17). But, somewhat paradoxically, Blair's invocation of the current philosophical orthodoxy concerning progress is too close to the letter and not to the spirit of his peers' accounts. For Hume, Smith, and Rousseau – like Steuart, Ferguson, Dunbar, and others later – in fact cast the shadow of unknowability and of uncertainty over every one of their statements, and over the whole intellectual exercise of conjectural history itself. This is the level of nuance, of sophistication and of totality the reigning epistemological orthodoxy dictates. Blair, by contrast, in common with Macpherson, invokes the whole intellectual worldview of contemporary scepticism but then proceeds as if, in the case of Ossian, it is not fully relevant.

Blair's *Dissertation* thus considers cultural artefacts such as *Ossian* alongside detailed expression of the tenets of contemporary scepticism, *but* does so at the same time as contending that such objects function as time capsules for past social and intellectual modes – themselves conceived in sceptical terms – that put their reader on epistemologically surer footing. Because this logic of literary criticism that Blair deploys is still in use (in a closely related form) today, we are seeing here how its early deployment relies on both sceptical and stadial terms. If the mind works differently in different social modes – so this logic goes – if 'notions and feelings' vary across time and space, then the very structure of social difference can be accessed through cultural artefacts, so long as the observer is able to analyse ideas with epistemological and political sophistication. Doing so, moreover, allows for a meeting of minds, as it were, across the divides of space and time, that is otherwise rarely possible, and that is therefore revelatory of large-scale cultural change. Blair's positivity regarding this method – his deviation from the correct sceptical postures of 'modesty', 'reserve' and 'suspended judgement' – must be recognized, however, to play down its limitations, as these are made visible by contemporary sceptical patterns of thought. First and foremost, elsewhere in contemporary thought the stadial hypothesis is registered as itself doubtful, as a convenient – and notably flattering – heuristic device, but as one that must, in all probability, simplistically schematize an in-fact unmanageable complexity.[72] This comprehensive, self-reflexive sense of doubt thus holds in check the constant human passion for certainty that Hume and others describe. In Blair's text, however, because stadial progress is taken as solidly, monolithically certain, the modes of social difference historical artefacts will reveal is already largely anticipated – and simplified. Blair expounds at length, for instance, on how '[e]very thing' in *Ossian*, 'presents to us the most simple and unimproved manners' (*Dissertation*, p. 17). This, in other words, is the same heuristic problem contemporary scepticism describes as the false allure of systems. Any heuristic scheme quickly becomes, because of the human passion for certainty, a trap for the human intellect. The wide contemporary knowledge of this exact epistemological problem is evidenced in Laurence Sterne's *Tristram Shandy*, of 1759. Tristram depicts his father as problematically 'systematical' by recapping, in extreme and satirical terms, the shared philosophical consensus on this issue: 'like all systematick [*sic*] reasoners, he would move both heaven and earth, and twist and torture every thing in nature to support his hypothesis'.[73]

The second, closely related problem Blair must play down is that of ideological bias, which is again a frequent presence in contemporary discussions of these issues, as we've seen. In Macpherson's Ossian commentary this issue was tidied away (not entirely satisfactorily) by the assertion that the translations being presented were so 'literal' as to transmit the original text in an unmediated form. Blair arguably takes even more liberties with this issue by claiming that the translation itself is a 'work [...] of genius', which 'proves the translator to have been animated with no small portion of Ossian's spirit' (*Dissertation*, p. 75). He also reports that he has 'been assured by persons skilled in the Galic [*sic*] tongue, who from their youth, were acquainted with many of these poems of Ossian' that the poems are translated with 'faithfulness and accuracy' (*Dissertation*, p. 75). Again, in other words, these statements work to claim that there is no issue at all with intercultural translation, even across the supposedly large stretch of time between the poems' composition and the 1760s. Instead, for Blair, the modern, 'commercial' mind can simply access the mind of the 'hunter', and can comprehend all of its patterns and assumptions, without any need for contextual information, for example. Once Blair himself, or his imagined reader, has the apparently certain knowledge of the

---

[72] This stance on the stadial categories has arguably been bolstered by Wengrow and Graeber's recent *The Dawn of Everything*, which uses decades of archaeological and anthropological evidence to contend that historical social change is fundamentally non-linear, with the supposed, one-way threshold between nomadic life and settled agriculture in fact being crossed and re-crossed countless times and in countless different ways.

[73] Sterne, *Tristram Shandy*, p. 38.

stages of human history, he or she can simply see that the poems plainly document the 'first of these periods'. And similarly there is no chance that the very terms in which Macpherson has rendered the ancient poetry colour, inflect or at all modify its nuances and details. Blair's claims, in his *Dissertation*, are therefore being made with a species of intercultural naivety – and political simplicity – that work against the epistemological rigour his references to contemporary scepticism generate. And yet these issues are by no means more modern methodological quibbles. Contemporary philosophy fully and repeatedly considers these traps of knowledge and certainty, and very often positions them as the constant limiting factors in all intellectual and historical inquiry, and as ones that must be acknowledged, and carefully negotiated, in any work of moral philosophy.

Blair and Macpherson's commentaries on the Ossian project must therefore be considered to represent a third and final position on the spectrum of epistemological accuracy visible in contemporary progress discussions. Both figures allude at length to the contemporary orthodoxies of scepticism, and strategically signal their participation in the same knowledge project that scepticism dictates. But both figures also proceed, nevertheless, further towards certainty than that tradition allows, and in this sense infuse their claims with more unevidenced, simplistic, lay conceptions of knowledge and politics. Their commentaries are assertions that the limitations on human knowledge contemporary scepticism describes do not fully pertain in the case of Ossian, and therefore that the poetry they are presenting offers a genuine opportunity for certain knowledge. Even more directly than Millar, then, whose 1781 text claimed that the careful, philosophically informed weighing of a huge terrain of evidence could produce certainty with regard to stadial progress, Macpherson and Blair assert that readers of Ossian are indeed viewing, directly and with full clarity, the mental and social worlds of early society.

Conclusion

The approach this study has taken to its three examples of mid to late eighteenth-century progress discussions offers an alternative means of classifying this field, and of accounting for its political variations, to those dominant in recent criticism. Contrary to David Spadafora's assertion that such writing evidences a broadly shared belief in the progressive nature of human social history; and contrary to Roxann Wheeler's additional claims that contemporary stadial history is 'undergirded' by beliefs in human 'perfectibility' and in commercial Europe being 'the best place on earth'; we have seen here that eighteenth-century analyses of progress and of civilization can be understood as variations from a core body of sceptical tenets regarding the impossibility of making reliable judgements on such matters. What may seem, on the surface, to be a range of idiosyncratic 'beliefs' regarding social evolution, in other words, is better understood, I contend, as an array of possible negotiations of what Anton Matytsin describes as the unanswerable status of sceptical analysis, at the mid-point of the eighteenth century. Matytsin's claim refers primarily to contemporary French intellectual culture. The analysis of this study, however, evidences its equal applicability to Scottish thought. What John Regan terms stadial history's consistent 'nuances' are therefore explained here as structurally necessary ambivalences the contemporary climate of philosophical scepticism generates. Political certainties, one way or another, concerning questions of social progress are not fully possible, in this epistemological climate, because contemporary scepticism pinpoints the manifold difficulties surrounding the evidentiary basis of all knowledge, and highlights how the evidence of social history is an especially problematic case.

To follow the reigning sceptical orthodoxies regarding historical knowledge, in the mid eighteenth century, is thus to find the issue of whether 'progress' is a satisfactory heuristic device for human history to be largely moot. (The contemporary sceptical proto-psychology, however, describes how the human mind is driven, nevertheless, to pursue such inquiries, so strong is its thirst for the feelings of knowledge and of certainty – even to those who recognize knowledge's nature as radically limited surmise and analogy.) This is why we have seen, in Dunbar's thought, what is also to be found in Smith and in Ferguson: an acknowledgement of the impasse inquiries into 'progress' face, and a promotion, instead, of a sophisticated form of suspended judgement on such matters, together with a focus on suggesting how existing institutions could become – through such self-reflexive analysis – positive forces for moral good. This stance therefore stands at one end of a spectrum of positions it is possible to take up on matters of progress, in the mid to late eighteenth century. To move away from this position, therefore, is to move towards more blanket, less critical, more simplistic, lay-knowledge, and lay-politics. This is the set of impulses and ideas that contemporary philosophy characterizes as 'instinctive', as biased and prejudiced, but also as an unstoppable and transhistorical stance. We have seen two instances of such movement between self-reflexive scepticism and innate, seemingly certain judgement here. On the one hand, James Macpherson and Hugh Blair move towards a mode of cultural primitivism in which 'early' social life is both supposedly fully recoverable, and supposedly throws modern commercial society in to the shade. On the other, John Millar moves towards a mode of colonialist hubris regarding the heights of 'civilization' contemporary Europe has achieved. In both these instances, however, we have seen that such gestures require considerable deviations from the dominant sceptical logics of moral philosophy, especially as these play out in natural, conjectural history. The fact that Macpherson, Blair, and Millar all refer, extensively, to the same shared body of sceptical tenets – even as they seek to sidestep them – is evidence of that epistemological mode's centrality to contemporary culture, and of its considerable influence.

The new understanding of eighteenth-century progress discussions constructed here is thus one in which – perhaps paradoxically to modern eyes – doubt over the very possibility of isolating knowledge in this sphere is part and parcel of such inquiries themselves. The terms 'speculation' and 'conjecture', recall, are ones that advertise their subtle and vexed epistemological status, but nevertheless assert that their contents may be useful, or at the very least entertaining. The self-reflexivity built in to these terms points towards a central political orientation of these progress discussions we have not yet picked out, moreover. This is that all the texts considered here assert, in one way or another, that their readers must recognize the doubtful nature of the whole intellectual exercise of understanding social history. Even Millar and Macpherson stress this. And this consistent reminder is also a call for sophisticated self-consciousness on the part of their readers. The human mind has 'instinctive propensities' that push it towards arrogance and intercultural hubris, all of the authors considered here say, in one form or another. Millar, for example, remarks on this as follows:

> Not all the allurements of European luxury could bribe a Hottentot to resign that coarse manner of life which was become habitual to him; and we may remark, that the 'maladie du pays', which has been supposed peculiar to the inhabitants of Switzerland, is more or less felt by the inhabitants of all countries[.] (*Ranks*, p. 179)

And what this means is that the intellectual enterprise of attempting an account of social evolution is one that, at its very heart, serves to engender critical and intercultural self-reflexivity in its readers. To make observations on, and to explore the parameters of, the biases implicit in quotidian knowledge, is, in other words, to generate political meta-knowledge for these texts' readers. Further, to include accounts of the shared, contemporary sceptical proto-psychology, as all the authors considered here do, in their opening framings of their inquiries, is to promote awareness of the largely illusory and unmoored nature of the human knowledge of social history. Arguably the central intellectual and political gestures of all the writing considered here are thus to promote critical self-reflection and to exemplify how the practices of 'speculative' reasoning might be applied to quotidian, instinctive beliefs. These texts are united, therefore – despite their variations in claims – in a political project of making a distinction between unthinking bias, including false certainty, and a more subtle and epistemologically informed, provisional and lightly held mode of political thinking. Even Macpherson, who occupies the position furthest towards lay-knowledge in my analysis, observes, repeatedly, that the human mind's instinctive bias hides the many positive qualities of the past, and that for his readership to reflect on this from within modernity is to expand their intellectual and spiritual horizons. This is why poetry is configured, by Blair, as 'contribut[ing]', highly influentially, 'to exalt the publick manners':

> Some of the qualities indeed which distinguish a Fingal, moderation, humanity, and clemency, would not probably be the first ideas of heroism occurring to a barbarous people: But no sooner had such ideas begun to dawn on the minds of poets, than, as the human mind easily opens to the native representations of human perfection, they would be seized and they would enter into their panegyricks; they would afford materials for succeeding bards to work upon, and improve; they would contribute not a little to exalt the publick manners. (*Dissertation*, pp. 14–15)

To follow the train of thinking cultural artefacts offer – in this formulation anticipating Percy Shelley's claim that poets are 'the unacknowledged legislators of the world'[74] – is to open one's mind to alternative social and political realities, and to perform a mode of thinking liberated from one's instinctual, unthinking bias.

To step back even further from the details of the analysis performed in this study, I want to reiterate that my reframing of eighteenth-century thought concerning progress with the procedures and claims of contemporary scepticism necessitates moving away from any identification of individual authors' 'beliefs' or 'opinions' on social development. This reframing can help us deal with the seeming contradiction, whereby every contemporary travel narrative, including Samuel Hearne's quoted earlier, *and* every text of stadial history or moral philosophy referred to in my analysis, both uses derogatory, prejudiced language for non-European peoples — 'savages', 'barbarians', etc. — but also, sometimes in the very same sentence, challenges the conventional prejudice that those terms support. Smith's phrasing, in Book V of the *Wealth of Nations*, is a case in point: 'In those barbarous societies, as they are called, every man, it has already been observed, is a warrior' (*WN*, II: 783). (Smith has just lamented the loss of martial virtue in commercial modernity.) This apparent contradiction, which is very widespread indeed in eighteenth-century thought, means that it seems to me an untenable position to claim that instances of derogatory

---

[74] Shelley, *A Defence of Poetry*, p. 701.

language ultimately demonstrate their author's support for commercial modernity, or belief in stadial progress and 'civilization'. Instead, the present analysis is an attempt to recover an alternative paradigm active in contemporary thought on questions of social difference. In this paradigm, sceptical moral philosophy identifies the condition of human knowledge as inevitable false surmise, and demonstrates, in all its different generic applications — metaphysics, political economy, astronomy, history, and so on — how such false simplifications manifest themselves. In Smith's posthumous handling of astronomy, for instance, he clarifies that the human mind cannot help but take the analogous, incomplete approximations of that field's explanations as if they were the real material grasping of how the universe works. Further — and again representative of what takes place in contemporary stadial history — Smith draws attention to his own mind's liability in this sense:

> And even we, while we have been endeavouring to represent all philosophical systems as mere inventions of the imagination, to connect together the otherwise disjointed and discordant phenomena of Nature, have insensibly been drawn in, to make use of language expressing the connecting principles of this one, as if they were the real chains which Nature makes use of to bind together her several operations. ('Astronomy', p. 105)

For our present purposes, what this means is that the sceptical philosopher, across French and Scottish contemporary thought, consistently and repeatedly configures himself as also partaking in the same unthinking, instinctive biases as his contemporaries. He also, repeatedly, configures every attempt at knowledge, including his own, to be radically limited by the same impasses scepticism identifies. The equivalent mental bias to the false materiality of astronomy in the field of stadial history is clearly, as Smith and Dunbar's analysis amply demonstrates, bias towards one's own society's superiority, most often in racialized terms. The careful distinction Hume and his counterparts in France make between how it is 'natural' for humans to think, and what the sceptical analysis and deconstruction of knowledge shows us is actually happening in that process, may, in other words, be deployed as a powerful tool for analysis, in contemporary moral philosophy. But it is by no means an exemption, for the philosopher himself, from non-sceptical surmise. The latter, indeed, is instead consistently configured as a terrain of thought from which it is a constant struggle to break free.

The modern intellectual apparatus, I contend, that allows us to handle this paradoxical situation best, is textual analysis. For texts, as they have been theorized in waves of scholarship across the twentieth and twenty-first centuries, are not pure expressions of belief, controlled by, and representing, their authors with total clarity. Instead they embody, manifest, and make legible all the complexities, contradictions and failings of human systems of thought and attempts at comprehension. The present study's claims regarding the texts of Scottish stadial history stand at a considerable distance from the project of Spadafora or Wheeler, therefore. To identify the incompatible textual currents side by side in Millar's 1781 *Distinction of Ranks*, for example, is not to move towards any judgement on Millar's 'belief' or 'opinions', or to opine on whether his arguments are factually correct, or indeed to pass judgement on whether there is an objective basis on which to rank civilization. Rather, this study asserts that the complex, contradictory, confused project of stadial history can only be seen correctly in the light of the contemporary scepticism that informs and structures its whole project; and that doing so allows us to recognize that its statements do not confirm to later models of evidence-based 'scientific' factuality, and cannot be subjected to the questions regarding truth and what is correct, which that later set of assumptions generates.

Finally, then, we must note that this identification of the interconnected and vexed features of contemporary progress analyses, and their origin in contemporary scepticism, complicates, significantly, the extent to which this body of thought simply underpins later, further-racialized, colonialist accounts of European supremacy over other peoples, and of the necessity of brutally imposing cultural and economic norms on other societies. While Millar's 1781 'Introduction' to his *Ranks* is the closest these texts come to expressing this body of ideas, even in that case there remains abundant textual evidence of the more subtle political logic of 'natural history', as well as all the more complex lines of interpretation in the body of Millar's text itself. If we were to add into consideration an even wider selection of texts, it is striking that – as I have referred to as means of comparison here – the most influential philosophers of the Scottish Enlightenment – Hume, Smith, and Ferguson, for example – all occupy orthodox sceptical positions on epistemological matters, at this historical moment, and that this stance plays out in their analyses of progress and civilization in much the same way as it does in Dunbar's *Essays*. Overall, therefore, it seems warranted to claim that mid to late eighteenth-century Scottish thought considering social difference stands at a considerable remove from later colonialist ideologies. At the centre of this difference is the epistemologically subtle and complex status of 'conjecture' and of 'speculation', both of which should be understood to embody – and to perform – the sceptical deconstruction of lay knowledge, as this is repeatedly expressed in contemporary thought.

Bibliography

Primary Sources

Anon., 'System', trans. Stephen J. Gendzier, *The Encyclopedia of Diderot & d'Alembert Collaborative Translation Project* (Ann Arbor: Michigan, 2009), online, last accessed 30 November 2020, http://hdl.handle.net/2027/spo.did2222.0001.321 [n. p.].

d'Alembert, Jean-Baptiste le Rond, 'Preliminary Discourse', *The Encyclopedia of Diderot & d'Alembert Collaborative Translation Project*, trans. Richard N. Schwab & Walter E. Rex (Ann Arbor: Michigan, 2009), online, last accessed 30 November 2020, http://hdl.handle.net/2027/spo.did2222.0001.083, [n. p.].

Blair, Hugh, *A Critical Dissertation on the Poems of Ossian, the Son of Fingal* (London: T. Becket & P. A. De Hondt, 1763).

Dunbar, James, *Essays on the History of Mankind in Rude and Cultivated Ages* (London: W. Strahan, 1780).

Ferguson, Adam, *An Essay on the History of Civil Society 1767*, ed. D. Forbes (Edinburgh: Edinburgh University Press, 1966).

Hearne, Samuel, *A Journey from Prince of Wales's Fort in Hudson's Bay to the Northern Ocean* (London: A. Strahan, 1795).

Hume, David, *Enquiries Concerning Human Understanding and Concerning the Principles of Morals*, eds. L. A. Selby-Bigge & P. H. Nidditch (Oxford: Clarendon, 1975).

— *A Treatise of Human Nature*, eds. L. A. Selby-Bigge & P. H. Nidditch (Oxford: Clarendon, 1978).

Macpherson, James, *Fragments of Ancient Poetry Collected in the Highlands of Scotland and Translated from the Galic or Erse Language* (Edinburgh: G. Hamilton & J. Balfour, 1760).

— *Fingal: An Ancient Epic Poem in Six Books* (Dublin: Richard Fitzsimons, 1763).

— *Temora, An Ancient Epic Poem in Eight Books* (London: T. Becket & P. A. De Hondt, 1763).

Mill, John Stuart, *Principles of Political Economy*, ed. V. W. Bladen, 2 Vols (London: Routledge, 1965).

Millar, John, *The Origin of the Distinction of Ranks; or, an Inquiry into the Circumstances Which Give Rise to Influence and Authority in the Different Members of Society*, ed., Aaron Garrett (Indianapolis: Liberty Fund, 2006).

Ricardo, David, *Principles of Political Economy*, ed. P. Sraffa, 2 Vols. (Cambridge: Cambridge University Press, 1951).

Rousseau, Jean-Jacques, *A Discourse on Inequality*, ed. M. Cranston (London: Penguin, 1984).

Shelley, Percy, *A Defence of Poetry*, *The Major Works*, eds. Z. Leader & M. O'Neill (Oxford: Oxford University Press, 2009).

Smith, Adam, *An Inquiry into the Nature and Causes of the Wealth of Nations*, eds. R. H. Campbell & A. S. Skinner, 2 Vols. (Indianapolis: Liberty Fund, 1976).

The Theory of Moral Sentiments, eds. D. D. Raphael & A. L. Macfie (Oxford: Clarendon Press, 1976).

'Report of 1762-3', in *Lectures on Jurisprudence*, eds. R. L. Meek, D. D. Raphael, & P. G. Stein (Oxford: Oxford University Press, 1978), pp. 1–394.

'Of the External Senses', in *Essays on Philosophical Subjects*, eds. W. P. D. Wightman & J. C. Bryce (Oxford: Oxford University Press, 1978), pp. 135–70.

'The History of Astronomy', in *Essays on Philosophical Subjects*, ed. W. P. D. Wightman & J. C. Bryce (Oxford: Oxford University Press, 1978), pp. 33–105.

'History of Ancient Logics and Metaphysics', in *Essays on Philosophical Subjects*, ed. W. P. D. Wightman & J. C. Bryce (Oxford: Oxford University Press, 1908), pp. 118–32.

Sterne, Laurence, *Tristram Shandy*, ed. H. Anderson (London: Norton, 1980).

Steuart, James, *Inquiry into the Principles of Political Oeconomy: Being an Essay on the Science of Domestic Policy in Free Nations*, 2 Vols. (London: A. Millar & T. Cadell, 1767).

Stewart, Dugald, 'Account of the Life and Writings of Adam Smith, L. L. D.', in *The Works of Adam Smith* (London: T. Cadell & W. Davies, 1812), pp. 403–78.

Voltaire [François-Marie Arouet], 'History', trans. Jeremy Caradonna, *The Encyclopedia of Diderot & d'Alembert Collaborative Translation Project* (Ann Arbor: Michigan, 2009), online, last accessed 30 November 2020, http://hdl.handle.net/2027/spo.did2222.0000.088 [n. p.].

Secondary Sources

Adelman, Richard, *Idleness & Aesthetic Consciousness, 1815–1900* (Cambridge: Cambridge University Press, 2018).

Doubtful Knowledge: Scepticism and the Birth of Political Economy (forthcoming).

Finlay, Christopher J., 'Rhetoric and Citizenship in Adam Ferguson's *Essay on the History of Civil Society*', *History of Political Thought*, 27:1 (Spring, 2006): 27–49.

Foucault, Michel, *The Order of Things: An Archaeology of the Human Sciences* (New York: Vintage, 1994).

Garrett, Aaron, 'Millar's Preface to the First Edition', in John Millar, *The Origin of the Distinction of Ranks*, ed. Aaron Garrett (Indianapolis: Liberty, 2006), p. 284.

Graeber, David, *Debt: The First 5,000 Years* (London: Melville, 2011).

Griswold, Charles, *Adam Smith and the Virtues of Enlightenment* (Cambridge: Cambridge University Press, 1999).

'Philosophy and Skepticism', in *Adam Smith and the Virtues of Enlightenment* (Cambridge: Cambridge University Press, 1999), pp. 147–78.

Laursen, John Christian & Gianni Paganini, 'Introduction' to *Skepticism and Political Thought in the Seventeenth and Eighteenth Centuries*, eds. J. C. Laursen & G. Paganini (Toronto: Toronto University Press, 2015), pp. 3–16.

Lucas, Jospeh S., 'The Course of Empire and the Long Road to Civilization: North American Indians and Scottish Enlightenment Historians', *Explorations in Early American Culture*, 4 (2000): 166–90.

Matytsin, Anton, *The Spectre of Skepticism in the Age of Enlightenment* (Baltimore: Johns Hopkins University Press, 2016).

Matytsin, Anton & Jeffrey D. Burston (eds.), *The Skeptical Enlightenment: Doubt and Certainty in the Age of Reason* (Liverpool: Liverpool University Press, 2019).

Moore, Dafydd, 'Heroic Incoherence in James Macpherson's *The Poems of Ossian*', *Eighteenth-Century Studies*, 34:1 (2000): 43–59.

Palmeri, Frank, *State of Nature, Stages of Society: Enlightenment Conjectural History and Modern Social Discourse* (New York: Columbia University Press, 2016).

Percy, Thomas, *Reliques of Ancient English Poetry* (1767).

Perelman, Michael, *The Invention of Capitalism: Classical Political Economy and the Secret History of Primitive Accumulation* (London: Duke University Press, 2000).

Plassart, Anna, '"Scientific Whigs"? Scottish Historians on the French Revolution', *Journal of the History of Ideas*, 74:1 (January, 2013): 93–114.

Popkin, Richard H., 'David Hume and the Pyrrhonian Controversy', *The Review of Metaphysics*, 6:1 (1952): 65–81.

'Did Hume or Rousseau Influence the Other?' *Revue Internationale de Philosophie*, 32:124/5 (1978): 297–308.

Regan, John, 'Ambiguous Progress and Its Poetic Correlatives: Percy's *Reliques* and Stadial History', *ELH* 81:2 (Summer, 2014): 615–34.

Rosenberg, Jordana & Chi-ming Yang, 'The Dispossessed Eighteenth Century', *The Eighteenth Century* 55:2/3 (Summer/Fall, 2014): 137–52.

Schabas, Margaret & Carl Wennerlind, *A Philosopher's Economist: Hume and the Rise of Capitalism* (Chicago: Chicago University Press, 2020).

Schliesser, Eric, *Adam Smith: Systematic Philosopher and Public Thinker* (Oxford: Oxford University Press, 2017).

Sebastiani, Silvia, *The Scottish Enlightenment: Race, Gender, and the Limits of Progress*, trans. Jeremy Carden (New York: Palgrave Macmillan, 2013).

Sher, Richard B., 'Blair, Hugh', *Oxford Dictionary of National Biography*, https://doi.org/10.1093/ref:odnb/2563, last accessed 9 July 24.

Siskin, Clifford, *System: The Shaping of Modern Knowledge* (Boston, MA: MIT Press, 2016).

Spadafora, David, *The Idea of Progress in Eighteenth-Century Britain* (New Haven: Yale University Press, 1990).

Wengrow, David & David Graeber, *The Dawn of Everything: A New History of Humanity* (London: Allen Lane, 2021).

Wheeler, Roxan, *The Complexion of Race: Categories of Difference in Eighteenth-Century British Culture* (Philadelphia: University of Pennsylvania Press, 2000).

Wood, Paul, 'Aberdeen Philosophical Society', *Oxford Dictionary of National Biography*, https://doi.org/10.1093/ref:odnb/95092, last accessed 8 July 24.

Acknowledgements

I would like to express my gratitude to Peter Kitson for his encouraging comments on the ideas under consideration in this Element, to colleagues at Sussex including Tom F. Wright and Catherine Packham for the stimulating discussions and collaborations that informed my thinking here, and to my Sussex MA students over the last few years, in particular Redmond Kerr, for sharing and contributing to my enthusiasm for rethinking eighteenth-century 'conjecture'.

Cambridge Elements =

Eighteenth-Century Connections

Series Editors
Eve Tavor Bannet
University of Oklahoma

Eve Tavor Bannet is George Lynn Cross Professor Emeritus, University of Oklahoma and editor of *Studies in Eighteenth-Century Culture*. Her monographs include *Empire of Letters: Letter Manuals and Transatlantic Correspondence 1688–1820* (Cambridge, 2005), *Transatlantic Stories and the History of Reading, 1720–1820* (Cambridge, 2011), and *Eighteenth-Century Manners of Reading: Print Culture and Popular Instruction in the Anglophone Atlantic World* (Cambridge, 2017). She is editor of *British and American Letter Manuals 1680–1810* (Pickering & Chatto, 2008), *Emma Corbett* (Broadview, 2011) and, with Susan Manning, *Transatlantic Literary Studies* (Cambridge, 2012).

Markman Ellis
Queen Mary University of London

Markman Ellis is Professor of Eighteenth-Century Studies at Queen Mary University of London. He is the author of *The Politics of Sensibility: Race, Gender and Commerce in the Sentimental Novel* (1996), *The History of Gothic Fiction* (2000), *The Coffee-House: a Cultural History* (2004), and *Empire of Tea* (co-authored, 2015). He edited *Eighteenth-Century Coffee-House Culture* (4 vols, 2006) and *Tea and the Tea-Table in Eighteenth-Century England* (4 vols 2010), and co-editor of *Discourses of Slavery and Abolition* (2004) and *Prostitution and Eighteenth-Century Culture: Sex, Commerce and Morality* (2012).

Advisory Board
Linda Bree, *Independent*
Claire Connolly, *University College Cork*
Gillian Dow, *University of Southampton*
James Harris, *University of St Andrews*
Thomas Keymer, *University of Toronto*
Jon Mee, *University of York*
Carla Mulford, *Penn State University*
Nicola Parsons, *University of Sydney*
Manushag Powell, *Purdue University*
Robbie Richardson, *University of Kent*
Shef Rogers, *University of Otago*
Eleanor Shevlin, *West Chester University*
David Taylor, *Oxford University*
Chloe Wigston Smith, *University of York*
Roxann Wheeler, *Ohio State University*
Eugenia Zuroski, *MacMaster University*

About the Series
Exploring connections between verbal and visual texts and the people, networks, cultures and places that engendered and enjoyed them during the long Eighteenth Century, this innovative series also examines the period's uses of oral, written and visual media, and experiments with the digital platform to facilitate communication of original scholarship with both colleagues and students.

Cambridge Elements

Eighteenth-Century Connections

Elements in the Series

Eighteenth-Century Illustration and Literary Material Culture: Richardson, Thomson, Defoe
Sandro Jung

Making Boswell's Life of Johnson: An Author-Publisher and His Support Network
Richard B. Sher

Pastoral Care through Letters in the British Atlantic
Alison Searle

The Domino and the Eighteenth-Century London Masquerade: A Social Biography of a Costume
Meghan Kobza

Paratext Printed with New English Plays, 1660–1700
Robert D. Hume

The Art of the Actress
Fashioning Identities

A Performance History of The Fair Penitent
Elaine McGirr

Labour of the Stitch: The Making and Remaking of Fashionable Georgian Dress
Serena Dyer

Early English Periodicals and Early Modern Social Media
Margaret J. M. Ezell

Reading with the Burneys: Patronage, Paratext, and Performance
Sophie Coulombeau

On Wonder
Tita Chico

The Epistemologies of Progress
Richard Adelman

A full series listing is available at: www.cambridge.org/EECC

For EU product safety concerns, contact us at Calle de José Abascal, 56–1°,
28003 Madrid, Spain or eugpsr@cambridge.org.

www.ingramcontent.com/pod-product-compliance
Lightning Source LLC
LaVergne TN
LVHW020352260326
834688LV00045B/1679